Emerging Defence, Maritime and Aerospace Technologies

Emerging Defence, Maritime and Aerospace Technologies

Compiled & Edited by

Commander (Dr) Jayakrishnan N Nair
(Retd, Indian Navy)

HOW ACADEMICS
an imprint of Highlyy Publishing LLP

in association with

DRaS

ISBN: 978-93-95522-18-2 (Hardback)
First Published : 2023

Cataloging in Publication Data--DK
Courtesy: D.K. Agencies (P) Ltd. <docinfo@dkagencies.com>
Emerging defence, maritime and aerospace technologies / [editor], Commander (Dr) Jaykrishnan N Nair.
pages cm
ISBN 9789395522182 (hardback)
1. Military weapons--Technological innovations--India. 2. Military art and science--Technological innovations--India. I. Nair, Jaykrishnan N., 1969- editor.
LCC U162.E44 2023 | DDC 623.3 23

Published by : HOW ACADEMICS
an imprint of Highlyy Publishing LLP

Correspondence Address : 4/30 A II Floor, Double Storey Buildings
Vijay Nagar, Delhi-110009
Editorial: +91 9811026449
Sales : +91 9999953412
Email: info@howacademics.com
Website: www.howacademics.com

Printed in India

Foreword

The challenges of the military technology revolution are multifold and dynamic, bringing disruptions in military affairs. With globalisation and the technology boom, a new term 'Geo-technologies' has emerged which has become a tool of strategic competition and power play. At the centre of this contest is technology, a driver for economic, political, diplomatic and military power. This current technology tsunami will impose the greatest challenges to the military leaders and warfighters to comprehend, adapt and optimise their force multiplication effect. It would increasingly also mandate a joint force and dual-use character.

DRaS has evolved as a professional 'Think Tank' and a platform for quality research over its short evolution in the last two years. My association with DRaS dates back to 2020 as a Senior Adviser and I take pride in seeing its steady growth. DRaS website has currently around 400 articles and has a viewer-ship of 1.7 lakhs plus since inception and it shows a steady growth of its penetration into the research community igniting academic vigour.

The book *"Emerging Defence, Maritime and Aerospace Technologies"*, published by Defence Research and Studies (DRaS) is a welcomed step in the right direction. It addresses diverse technologies for the military with a focus on homegrown solutions and their impact on warfare, written by professional scholar warriors and subject matter experts. The book will serve well to enable understanding, adapting and exploiting niche technologies by the military, academia, research scholars and the larger global audience.

I compliment DRaS and its professional Team for this maiden publication and hone them to continue their pursuit of excellence in research and academics.

'Jai Hind'

01 Feb 2023

Lt Gen A B Shivane, PVSM, AVSM, VSM (RETD)

Former Director General Mechanised Forces, Indian Army

Editors' Note

The editors have rendered a sincere effort to include various articles covering a large spectrum of emerging technologies despite the constraints existing in publishing. Not many books have been published on emerging strategic technologies pertaining to defence, maritime and aerospace in India. The articles have covered a wide range of applications suiting to the requirement of academia and startups in the country.

The defence, maritime and aerospace industry is on the verge of a major expansion in this country for the next 20 years. The Government of India and academia have started giving more impetus to associated learning to boost up the growth in the defence sector. The 29 articles being presented in this book by scholarly veterans are a priceless contribution of their knowledge and wisdom which they have harnessed during their meritorious service in the armed forces and after leaving service. Most of the writers are currently in the academic profession and teaching at various universities in India.

The references for the articles being compiled are kept towards the end of this publication. Many images have been included by downloading from the public network by giving the courtesy to copyright owners. The articles are being compiled by the experienced editors of Defence Research and Studies (DRaS). Due diligence has been taken by editors to choose articles that are linked to emerging technologies in the field of defence, aerospace and maritime. The articles are curated by experienced editors without loosing the essence of the contents.

Introduction

1. The defence manufacturing sector in the country is set for a major leap. Export-Import policies associated with defence production and services are becoming more liberal. India has spent more than 80 billion dollars in the last 15 years for the military and is rated as the fifth largest spender on defence in the world. India is one of a leading importers of defence equipment and systems. There is a need to reverse the current situation by promoting domestic defence manufacturing in the coming years to support our growing economy.
2. Government of India has decided to curtail the imports of defence equipment and services by the year 2026/2027 towards becoming self-reliant. The Government has also set an annual export target for the defence sector at 5 billion USD by the year 2025. GOI has also established defence parks and defence corridors across the nation to help the startup ecosystem.
3. Aircraft and drone manufacturing sector of India is also on the verge of a major expansion. India has a matured missile technology, which has a huge potential for exports. IT enabled support systems for developing the defence and aerospace sector are experiencing major growth today. There is a need to hand hold the students by experienced retired armed force officers to help them venture into defence startups. This book is a small effort by veterans to support the endeavour of our Government and academia.
4. Defence Research and Studies (DRaS) is a 'Think Tank' formed by veterans of the armed forces. The 'DRaS innovations' trust has initiated an 'Edutech' venture, 'DRaS i Learning Systems', who is currently conducting courses on 'Defence Technology' (DT) at B Tech/UG level in Universities in online mode. This initiative is in line with the AICTE directives towards giving added impetus to Defence Technology (DT) in academia. This book would certainly help as a trigger for defence startups.
5. The exposure to emerging opportunities in defence, aerospace and maritime technology would certainly help the students and startups to explore the niche areas where they can go for successful startups which could benefit the nation too. Currently, Indian Armed Forces can give limited guidance to the academia due to security reasons, whereas the veterans can give the much needed support and guidance to the defence startups.
6. We hope this small endeavour would go a long way for our nation becoming a net exporter in defence equipment and associated technologies.

Contents

1. Pulse Detonation Engines- Future of Aerospace Propulsion

Cmde SL Deshmukh

Pulse Detonation Engines are economical and can revolutionise the power plants of military and civil aircraft.

With rapid technological advances in propulsion technology, the gamut of aerospace propulsion is undergoing a sea change. These days the rocket engines (air-breathers) are being used for aerospace propulsion purposes, but these are less efficient. Thus, efforts are in hand to find viable efficient alternatives for these.

Pulse Detonation Engine (PDE) is one such efficient engine that can replace rocket engines. Many countries including India are working on PDEs, the future of aerospace propulsion. Let us examine the concepts of the Pulse Detonation Engines, their functioning, recent advances, befits and problems related to PDEs, their future and current scenarios in India and Russia.

Concepts of Pulse Detonation Engines (PDE)

The Pulse Detonation Engines (PDEs) are being developed on an experimental basis (as of now) as propulsive devices that use supersonic detonation waves as a combustion mechanism. In theory, the PDEs offer numerous advantages over traditional gas turbine engines, including improved efficiency and reduced mechanical complexity. However, the concept has not matured yet and PDE designs still need to overcome significant hurdles in order to become a viable and efficient form of propulsion- which just a matter of time as research into PDE designs, engineering properties and potential is ongoing.

Traditional Gas Turbine Engines Vs Pulse Detonation Engines

In conventional jet engines (Fig-1.1), the air is compressed by means of a compressor and then mixed with fuel before the combustion stage, where the combustion is generally a subsonic process. The hot gases then drive a turbine, and in turn the compressor, before being accelerated through a nozzle thereby producing thrust.

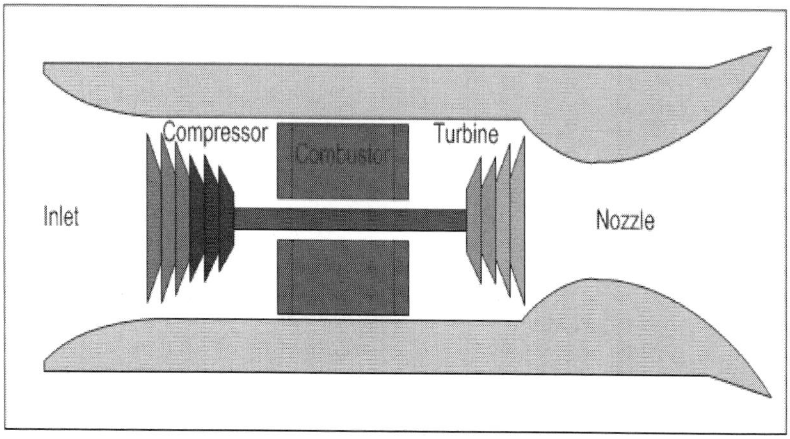

Fig 1.1 Conventional Turbo Jet Engine - Image Courtesy: Aerodynamics Research Center, University of Texas

The turbine engines cannot start from rest by themselves and require the use of a starter to get them to self-sustaining speeds. Conventional Jet engines follow the Brayton cycle, which requires the compression of air to high pressures before heat release is possible, thereby requiring the heavy compressor and turbine mechanisms.

In comparison, the Pulse Detonation Engines (PDEs) can operate theoretically from a standstill state up to a Mach number of 5. PDEs do not require heavy compressors, thereby reducing the overall weight and complexity of the engine. The geometry of PDEs is also simple, consisting essentially of a tube with control valves for fluid delivery. The detonation process delivers higher pressures and temperatures from the reaction and offers better efficiencies.

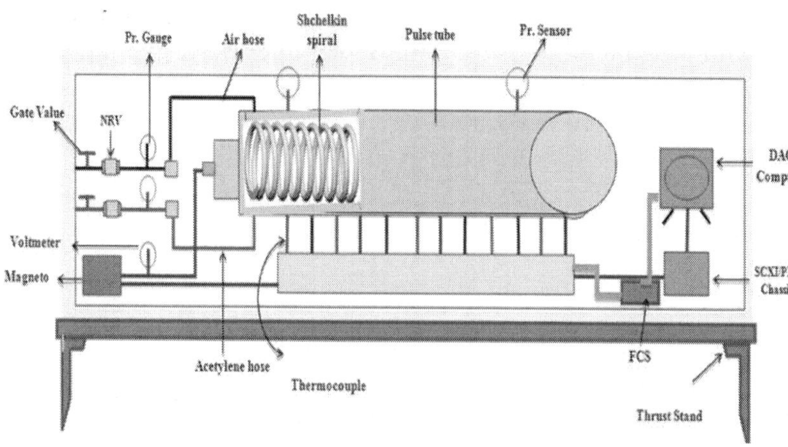

Fig: 1.2: Simplified schematic layout of PDE system - Image Courtesy: ResearchGate

The fundamental physics behind PDEs is rather simple. Combustion occurs in a shaft with valves or carefully crafted openings at each end so that gas can only pass one way through the device (Fig: 1. 2r). The fuel mixture in the chamber is ignited in such a way that it combusts and expands supersonically (detonation), sending a shock wave down the length of the chamber. Because the shock wave moves so rapidly, the rest of the fuel in the engine combusts before it has time to expand; thus, combustion occurs at approximately constant volume. A constant-volume combustion process releases more chemical potential energy as heat than the constant-pressure process found in conventional turbine engines (Cassidy, 2016).

The PDEs offer higher specific impulses than rockets and conventional air-breathing engines at all Mach numbers. Therefore, there are studies underway seriously attempting to integrate pulsed detonation mode of combustion within rockets and scramjet engines, which could combine the advantage of the boost in performance achieved from the *detonation process over the deflagration process** (*will be discussed later in the article).

PDEs essentially bridge the gap between the subsonic and the hypersonic regimes, after which scramjets and rockets take over. All of the above account for the explosion in the field of detonation and PDE research recently. This has led to the launch of several competing research programs with the aim of developing a working PDE system (ARC, 2014).

Difference Between Detonation and Deflagration

Detonation refers to the supersonic combustion process whereas deflagration is a subsonic combustion process. Almost all engines that burn fuel employ deflagration to release the energy contained within the fuels. In detonation, a shock wave compresses the gas which is then followed by the rapid release of heat and a sudden rise in pressure. As per Chapman-Jouguet theory, the detonation wave comprises a shock wave and a flame front. As the wave front passes through the gas, the gas is compressed and the chemical reaction is completed at the rear of the wave front. The detonation process is supposed to be more efficient than the deflagration (ARC ibid).

Historical Perspective- PDEs

Technologically, the Pulse Detonation Engines are the supersonic relatives of pulse-jet engines. Pulse- jets relied on intermittent, subsonic deflagration flames in a long tube to burn an injected fuel- oxidizer mixture. Pulse-jets emerged during World War II, as the propulsion system of the dreaded V-1 bombs. The performance of the pulse jets is limited by the constant pressure slow flame speed. In comparison, Detonation waves, a supersonic phenomenon, propagate at speeds in the thousands of meters per second, and can therefore be modelled as a constant volume process.

Serious research in the field of detonation propulsion systems began in the 1950s, at the University of Michigan. The novel idea of intermittent detonation gained traction in the 1980s as the Naval Postgraduate School (USA) investigated the design further. However, experimental work encountered a number of challenges, namely the difficulty with transitioning a subsonic deflagration wave (a flame) into a supersonic detonation wave, as well as properly mixing the fuel and oxidizer to produce a uniform detonation.

With the advancement in technology, the PDE concept has continued to garner academic research interest and PDE research is being attempted from a variety of angles, including computational fluid dynamics, experimental thermodynamics, as well as laser diagnostics. The prospects for PDEs are becoming brighter by the day (Cassidy, 2016a).

Recent Advances in PDE Technology

Many researchers working in the propulsion field have turned towards the pulse detonation engines, working with a combination of thermodynamics analysis, detonation initiation processes and deflagration to detonation wave transition devices as their main subject in the detonation combustion research area.

Research on rotating detonation engines and their application in aerospace turbo-machinery and performance assessment is also being progressed. These involve researches from the United States (Pratt and Whitney), Russia (United Engines Corporation), Japan and China, Germany, and Malaysia (HiREF, Universiti Teknologi). India (DRDO) has made a beginning in the field. The numbers of research publications have also increased significantly in recent years, thus making more material for further work. Researchers are hopeful of making a breakthrough, making PDEs commercially viable in the coming years (Pandey and Debnath, 2016).

Benefits and Problems Related to PDEs

Advantages

The simplicity of PDE's design is its undeniable virtue. Further, as the fluid combustion proceeds in the shock waves about 100 times faster than in conventional slow combustion (deflagration), this type of engine is theoretically distinguished by record power per unit of volume compared to all other types of thermal engines.

Apart from the high relative power the detonation engines potentially have other significant advantages. For example, during the cycle of detonation combustion is possible to achieve very high temperatures. But the combustion speed is also very high and nitrogen oxides do not have time to form, therefore the detonation engines are potentially environmentally friendly. The problem of cooling the combustion chamber is as well easier to solve. Despite the higher temperature and pressure in the detonation wavefront due to the transience of detonation combustion processes their impact on the engine's structure is less than that of classical motors. Usage of detonation combustion provides tangible advantages in the Liquid Rocket Engines as well (Bulat, 2014)

Limitations

Despite many advantages PDEs offer over conventional turbojet engines, PDEs are still away from commercial applications. There many technological limitations which need to be overcome. Some of them are (Valli and Jindal, 2014): -

a. One of the key barriers for an operational Pulse Detonation Engine lies in the difficulty to ignite the detonation wave in the engine in a reliable and controllable manner. This barrier is particularly critical for an application that involves hydrocarbon/air mixture. This is so because detonations are difficult to achieve within a practical length in hydrocarbon/air mixtures, which are less sensitive to detonation initiation.

b. Another difficulty is in optimizing the diameter of the detonation tube in a practical manner.

c. As of now, the Lengths of detonation tube required are quite large.

d. Cycle repetition frequency and Cell width are other issues which are creating barriers,

e. Research is still going on the most suitable materials for the manufacture of the PDE components.

Despite above limitations constant researches are going on the field of PDEs because of the vast potential they hold. Researchers are quite optimistic about the breakthroughs which would allow commercial usage of PDEs.

Future Outlook

Researchers feel that the pulse detonation engines have great potential to provide a significantly more efficient combustion cycle than deflagration-based engines. The application of this technology to turbines promises to increase the thermodynamic efficiency of these engines to previously unattainable levels.

The PDE- as a standalone engine also holds significant promise for both air-breathing and air-independent rocket propulsion, subject to further research on the following: -

a. Nozzles have been shown to have limited benefit to the thrust generated by PDEs.
b. Study of thrust to weight carrying out sufficient experimental work in vacuum conditions or microgravity conditions.
c. Determination of maximum equivalence ratio at which an RDE will operate.
d. Study on Triple points for determining the constraints, besides chemical composition.
e. Research on a mathematical relationship between the detonation cell width and the geometry requirements of the chamber.
f. Research on varying channel widths to determine what the optimal width would be for different design requirements.
g. Research to determine an appropriate chamber length and correlation with efficiency.

It has been demonstrated that the thrust produced by PDEs scales non-linearly with engine size, but they are not yet approaching the size required to replace most existing gas turbines. With many researchers working in the PDE field, it has been anticipated that the limitations could be overcome and PDEs could be scaled up sufficiently to provide the thrust levels offered by contemporary gas turbine engines, in due course of time (Shaw et al, 2018).

PDE Developed by Russia

It has been reported that Russia's United Engine Corporation (UEC) has completed the first stage of testing a pulse detonation engine (fig 1.3), which in the future can be used in advanced rocket and space systems, hypersonic aircraft and orbital space-planes. In some operating modes, the power plant has demonstrated up to a 50% increase in specific thrust when compared to conventional engines. ROSTEC Aviation Cluster has stated the following in relation to the PDE tests:

The first stage of testing the pulse detonation engine demonstrator has been successfully completed. It has shown the required performance characteristics. In some operation modes, the specific thrust was up to 50% higher than the performance of traditional power plants. This will prospectively increase the maximum range and payload mass of aircraft by 1.3–1.5 times. The design will be able to be applied, for example, on orbital space-planes, supersonic and hypersonic aircraft, and future-generation rocket and space systems.

Russia feels that Aircraft equipped with pulse detonation engines will have better flight dynamics and manoeuvrability. The engine type can be used to develop traditional rocket and air-jet propulsion systems or their support systems (Indiadefencenews, 2021).

Fig: 1.3 Russia's PDE - Image Courtesy: Defence World

PDE by DRDO

It has been reported that India's Defence Research and Development Organisation (DRDO) has developed a pulse detonation engine which has higher fuel efficiency than the gas turbine ones for cruise, anti-tank missile and unmanned aerial vehicles propulsion (fig 1.4).

Post-tests on the basic engine, DRDO's unit Terminal Ballistics Research Laboratory (TBRL) is currently working on an air-breathing multi-tube, multi-cycle pulse detonation engine. TBRL is working on an air-breathing multi-tube multi-cycle pulse detonation engine with an objective to develop an air-breathing Pulse Detonation Engine to generate 2.5 kN of thrust for a duration of 30 minutes.

As TBRL, for flying systems, detonation requires a long tube length to accommodate the required amount of energy input. TBRL has been working on a system to reduce the length of the engine so that it can be applied in systems like UAVs and other missiles system as well. A DRDP Paper on the subject pointed out that:

To reduce engine length, suitable devices are employed which reduce the length of the tube required for the transition from deflagration to detonation. A test rig was designed and established for conducting experiments with liquid fuel-air mixtures.

DRDO is hopeful of taking the research forward and achieving a breakthrough for providing PDE based equipment to Indian armed forces followed by commercial applications (defence world, 2017).

Fig: 1.4 - DRDO Developed PDE - Image Courtesy: Defence World

Conclusion

Technologically it has been anticipated that the PDEs would offer numerous advantages over current jet and rocket propulsion systems. But their practical development has met with numerous challenges, quite a few of which remain unsolved today.

PDE researchers feel that advances in this field have pushed the boundaries of engineering knowledge by fuelling the development of improved gas dynamic models and diagnostics while improving understanding of combustion science and fluid dynamics. They are hopeful of achieving the breakthrough to make PDEs both technologically and economically viable.

India (DRDO) has already taken the steps in this field and it is recommended that: -

a. A serious thought may be given to the continuation of the research in the PDE field and sufficient funds may be allocated for the work.

b. Though maybe given to building a synergetic approach with Russia to jointly develop technologically and financially viable PDEs. The Brahmos model may be considered for this project.

c. Threat from China's PDE program may be evaluated and parameters for research by DRDO be finalised based on the threat perception.

It is hoped that DRDO will rise to the occasion and make India Atmanirbhar in the field of Pulse Detonation Engines- a future of aerospace.

Jai Hind

2. Digital Underwater Data Storages

Dr Vijay Sakhuja

A container packed with servers and positioned 36 meters underwater off Orkney, northern Scotland has been successfully recovered by Microsoft after a two-year trial. Dubbed as Project Natick, the underwater data centre (UWDC) is powered by a local grid which supplies energy from renewable (wind, solar and other experimental marine energy systems) sources. Project Natick has also proven that data centre can be located underwater along the coast to support the rapidly increasing demand for cloud-based web services by businesses and people who are predicted to grow from the current 7.7 billion to 9.7 billion people in the next 30 years (Fig 2.1). It is useful to mention that over half of the global population is located within about 120 miles of the coast and numerous industries have been set up in coastal areas.

Fig 2.1 Lay out of Underwater Data Centre (PC-Data center dynamics)

There is also a comparable trend in the number of internet users worldwide up from 3.92 billion in 2018 to 4.13 billion in 2019. Similarly, the number of internet of things (IoT), a complex web of interconnected personal devices such as smartphones, smart domestic durables and appliances, the network of civil-military-economic-energy infrastructure, etc., around the world has grown to 22 billion at the end of 2018 and is projected to touch 50 billion by 2030.

Closely associated is the issue of transmission of data. It is estimated that nearly 90 per cent of the data transmission involves submarine cables which first made a debut in between England and France in 1850s. The submarine cable network has expanded rapidly and as of early 2020, there are approximately 406 submarine cables in service around the world. Furthermore, from a minuscule capacity of 10 words per minute in the 1850s, these submarine cables can transmit 40 gigabytes of data per strand of fibre and the carrying capacity can be expanded into the terabytes.

It is fair to assume that the future IoT would involve gigantic data (generated-shared) in zettabytes (ZB) and in the long run in yotobytes (YB), and stored in special central and compacted storage spaces called Data Centre. These would have racks of servers and transmit information to the wider internet service providers and users. For instance, the Microsoft Project Natick UWDC docking structure is 14.3 meters in length and 12.7 meters in width. It has 864 servers on 2 racks with a storage capacity of 27.6 petabytes (27,600 terabytes) which is "enough to store at least 5 million copies of **Finding Nemo**". (Fig 2.2).

Fig 2.2 Microsoft UW data centre PC- Youtube

The Data Centre is part of the digital infrastructure and needs hundreds of megawatts (MW) of power to run the servers, supporting systems such as monitoring equipment, lighting, etc. These generate enormous amounts of heat that can potentially degrade its efficiency, the operational life of the processor, and in extreme cases even destroying it. This necessitates cooling systems which can be energy guzzlers. It is likely that by 2025 Data Centres will consume nearly 33% of global electricity production and the cooling process could cost as much as an estimated US$ 1.4 billion in electricity. Furthermore, Data Centres are potential aggravators of climate change and according to a study, during 2010-2015 the global digital industry was responsible for 1.4% of global emissions.

A combination of carbon-negative and proximity to submarine cables/users has encouraged mega technology companies like Google and Microsoft to explore UWDC. In 2009, Google patented a "water-based data centre detailing a floating data centre, complete with an energy supply fed by a wind-powered cooling system and wave-powered generator system using seawater". Digital service providers have an ever-increasing demand for bandwidth for streaming audio-video-photos and other data. Netflix, YouTube and Web-based media streaming, the three major users (as of September 2019) of global traffic take up nearly 34.1% of the traffic and are investing in submarine cable systems by directly setting up new networks.

At another level, UWDC attracts stringent underwater requirements of being 'resistant to seismic activity, flooding, and other types of natural disasters and the design of the Data Centre should be such that it can be expanded. It should be efficient in terms of cost of operations as also close to a location that offers cheap power source to make it more affordable. Another important consideration for UWDC location is fibre networks which should be near the end-user to reduce latency.

In Singapore, Keppel Data Centres and Toll Group plan to install a floating data centre at the Loyang Offshore Supply Base. It is expected to be 'environmentally-friendly and resource-efficient' and would use seawater for cooling. It is particularly significant for Singapore, an island state, as it will 'free up valuable land for other urban uses, making it a particularly attractive proposition for land-scarce cities.

By all counts, the market trends with regard to UWDC are very promising. Besides Microsoft and Goggle, new projects by other digi-tech companies can be expected. They will, however, have to keep in mind that these have low-carbon-footprint, are in close vicinity to users, provide low-latency in connectivity for a high-quality experience as also do not impact on the underwater environment-ecology.

3. Augmenting Naval and Maritime ISR through IR 4.0 Technologies

Dr Vijay Sakhuja

SpaceX has added 60 new satellites to the Starlink internet constellation, an internet service project which aims to provide broadband services across the globe. Also, it's booster stage reusable rocket which packs more than 1.7 million pounds of thrust, was successfully recovered after a 'smooth touchdown' in the Atlantic Ocean by SpaceX's drone ship. According to Elon Musk, the founder of the SpaceX, his company has plans to launch nearly 12,000 satellites into orbit to provide high-speed broadband internet at locations where access is "unreliable, expensive, or completely unavailable" (Fig 3.1).

Fig 3.1 Starlink Satellites PC:Flying Magazine

Meanwhile, SpaceX has received orders from the US Space Development Agency (SDA) for satellites that can track and provide early warnings of hypersonic missile launches. The satellites are part of the SDA's Tracking Layer which will work in conjunction with the proposed Transport Layer (constellation of between 300 and 500 satellites) and will provide "low-latency military data and connectivity worldwide" to military assets. Earlier, in July, SpaceX launched Anasis-2 military communications satellite for South Korea

Fig 3.1 Launch Pad PC: SpaceX

Satellites have been in the inventory of modern militaries and used for navigation, accurate delivery of ordnance over long distances, and intelligence, surveillance and reconnaissance (ISR) tasks. The two Gulf Wars and the global war on terror demonstrated that satellites were game changers and facilitated accurate targeting of terrorists and their hideouts with little collateral damage. However, satellites attract a very high price tag and it is expensive to launch these notwithstanding the fact that these days it is possible to put multiple units into orbit using single and reusable rocket as has been demonstrated by the SpaceX programme (Fig 3.2).

Solar Powered UAVs (SPUAV) too are the leading technologies in the defence aerospace industry and are gaining popularity. These can be positioned in 'Near Space' in which aircraft do not fly, no satellite is positioned, and fuel-powered UAVs are unable to operate due to thin air which hampers the functioning of the engine. This area is a 'space desert' and has remained underutilized; however, it is now being populated with sub-orbital rockets, high-altitude balloons which can easily jump into and out of near space. The SPUAVs can provide persistent satellite-like services. Besides, these are cheaper and do not require fuel. Being lighter, they can remain aloft for extended periods of time and therefore are cost-effective. These also fulfil many of the missions now assigned to satellites or to high-altitude aircraft, such as the U-2, or Global Hawk UAV.

What is perhaps significant is that the SPUAVs would operate above the weather, be inherently stealthy, and fly above the range of nearly all threats. The cameras at that high altitude can see for several hundred miles farther than with aerial photography and access to a given area is more flexible than with the infrequent pass made by remote sensing satellite.

It is possible to exploit SPUAVs for several other functions such as secure communications, internet, coastal surveillance, earth remote sensing and ISR. These could remain on station for months, far longer than traditional UAVs and these may even have a longer shelf-operational life when compared with certain satellites. A constellation of 40 or 50 SPUAVs can thus undertake seamless ISR operations of strategic civilian and military infrastructure, coastal security and environmental monitoring. Also, SPUAVs can provide stable cellular and internet services in developing countries where remote areas are in desperate need of digital connectivity.

In the maritime domain, the belief that the oceans and seas are so large that it is impossible to keep an eye on every inch of this enormous space has attracted the proverbial saying 'finding a needle in a haystack'. This limitation is a passé and it is fair to envision a future in which the celestial space would be overwhelmed by satellites, Near Space technologies and UAVs. These platforms will generate enormous amounts of ISR data which would need to be processed and put to operational use that can potentially overwhelm the humans.

The global community is fast exiting the 'age of information' that featured information and communication technologies (ICT); it is now entering a new world of "knowledge-based environment" driven by the Fourth Industrial Revolution (4IR) technologies that are smart and intelligent, use predictive-cognitive tools and algorithms, and drive autonomous, unmanned and remote-controlled platforms, robots and machines. Some of the frontline technologies of 4IR are Artificial Intelligence (AI), Machine Learning (ML), Big Data, cloud computing, Augmented Reality (AR), Quantum Computing, Cognitive Computing (CC) and Internet of Things (IoT) are gathering momentum and finding use in supporting ISR operations.

These would radically transform ISR landscape not only how we design and develop new ISR platforms, but also how to maximize outcomes. In particular, the tools of generating Maritime Domain Awareness through traditional sources such as the Automatic Identification System (AIS) and the long-range identification and tracking (LRIT), a satellite-based, real-time reporting mechanism for reporting the position of ships, shore-based Electro-optical systems and high definition radars would need to be upended with 4IR-enabled systems to overcome weakness such as AIS data manipulation, Global Navigation Satellite System (GNSS) spoofing and jamming attacks and cyber-attacks. The World Economic Forum's Global Risks Report 2020 has listed cyber-attacks on critical infrastructure as the fifth top risk in 2020 and has a reference to shipping. Besides, AI and ML can help analyze the entire synchronization networks, forewarns service degradation and prepare for potential maintenance of the GNSS thereby ensuring these vital services are not disrupted.

At another level, a robust AI-based MDA can potentially contribute to transparency across the seas and oceans by integrating multi-source data, analytics and advanced Cloud services, It is a promising technology to track vessels, determine the type of cargo, business behaviour of shipping companies including freight forwarders as also in countering crimes at sea, particularly Illegal, Unreported and Unregulated (IUU) fishing which is high on the agenda for debate and discussions at the level of the United Nations and regional maritime security arrangements.

4. Cube Satellites- Rocketry Simplified

Cdr (Dr) Jayakrishnan N Nair

The movie 'Rocketry' has given us a great insight into the professional life of rocket scientists in India. The development of the 'Vikas Rocket Engine' by the Indian Space Research Organisation (ISRO) is a great milestone. Lifting heavy payloads for interplanetary missions is a challenge for the nations in the launch vehicle business. However, a new trend has started in the production and launch of small satellites with standard dimensions of 10 centimetres and it is named as 'Cube Satellites'(Fig 4.1a). Any satellite weighing between 1 kg to 10 kg falls under the nano-satellite category. The majority of the cube satellites being fabricated and launched are nano-satellites and they need rocket engines consuming less fuel to take them to *Low Earth Orbit (*LEO). Many amateur players and universities are now getting into the business of cube satellites across the globe. More than one cubes from the multiples of 10 centimetres (U) for multiples of U to specify the overall size (Fig 4.1b)

Fig 4.1a 1U satellite (10x10x10 Cms)

Fig 4.1b 3U frame (10X10X30 Cms)

ISRO had scripted history by successfully launching a record number of 104 satellites on 15 Feb 2017 with the help of a single rocket from the launchpad in Sriharikota. This is the highest number of satellites ever launched in a single mission and is a world record. Apart from satellite Cartosat - 2, all the other satellites were nano-satellites, of which 96 belonged to the USA. M/s Antrix Corporation Limited (ACL) is a wholly owned subsidiary of ISRO under the Department of Space. ACL is the marketing arm of ISRO for the promotion and commercial exploitation of space products, technical consultancy services and transfer of technologies developed by ISRO. There is a huge opportunity waiting for ACL in the cube satellite space in coming years.

The 'Cubesat' concept has standardized the satellites and on-board systems. This standardisation and miniaturisation are helping the developing nations to venture into satellite missions at a lower cost. Technical universities and space startups around the globe are currently focussing on developing systems and technologies aiding nano-satellites. An average of 500 nano-satellite launches have been predicted for the year 2023 and 90% of these satellites would come under the nano category. These satellites once placed at LEO (200 - 2000 km height) would take roughly 90 minutes and 2 hours' time to orbit the earth once.

Advantages

There are many advantages for Cubesats compared to the bigger ones. The satellites are very affordable and easy to assemble and construct. Commercially of the shelf (COTS), systems can be used for on-board avionic systems and energy requirements. Cubesats require less cost to get launched and need very less time for manufacturing and testing. In fact, ready-made kits are currently available in the market to purchase and assemble the satellites. Since the overall cost of production and launching is less, the risk of losing one satellite may not matter much. The satellite can be programmed to re-enter the earth's atmosphere after the lifespan and can be burnt during the descent. The cost of fabrication and launch is coming down after every year and is becoming affordable for all developing nations to own.

Applications

A variety of applications have been explored and lined up for Cubesats. They are progressively taking over the applications of bigger satellites. The main constraint of Cubesat is the life span compared to the bigger satellites. Many agencies are currently working on extending the life of Cube satellites. Cubesats are now used for applications like remote sensing, imaging, earth observation, communications, surveillance, tethering at space, OTH communication, navigation conjoined with GPS, telemetry etc. This has become an ideal platform for testing and demonstrations. Universities and academia use them extensively for their research and studies. In fact, satellite services and applications will get democratised across the developing world in the coming years. Apart from the V/UHF bands, the satellites can communicate in S, C, X, Ku and Ka bands also. Optical communication links (100 Mbps to 1 Gbps) are also being used for downlinks and inter-planetary communication networks. Much-needed bandwidth requirements for downloading high-resolution imageries have been met by migrating to the optical spectrum.

Space Research

Testing and demonstration of applications specific to space is one area where Cubesat plays a leading role. Cost is the major factor here for short-listing Cubesat by space research agencies across the world. A wide range of applications like re-entry material testing, inspection of other satellites/ space stations, propulsion experiments, resolving temporal resolution, interplanetary missions, deep space exploration, and tracking other satellites are a few to be named.

Defence and Security applications

A variety of applications have been explored in the defence and security domain with the Cubesats. These include applications like tracking ballistic missiles, hypersonic missiles tracking, carrying space-based radar systems, data communication from remote battlefields/ oceans, weather warnings at remote places, target designation, damage assessment, operating in constellations or swarms, autonomous missile defence systems etc. Armed forces should take advantage of this opportunity since the cost benefits are huge compared to bigger satellites.

Energy and Propulsion

Fig 4.2 Solar Sail Propulsion PC: Tech Crunch

Power generation and management is one of the main constrain in extending the life of satellites, hence is applicable to Cubesats too. Life of the battery, size of the battery, energy-carrying capacity of the battery, power generated by the solar plant, energy distribution and management w.r. to the consumption of payload equipment, propulsion and movement in orbit post-launch are some major factors that could affect the overall life of Cubesats. The propulsion of these satellites between orbits is a challenge due to energy constraints. Propellant tanks with thrusters are to be inbuilt for intra-orbital movement (Fig 4.1). Solar sails are one of the best alternatives available for the movement of Cubesats after reaching orbit.

Promising Future

There is a huge opportunity for our M/s Antrix Corporation Limited (ACL) of ISRO to cash in and find resources for their future space endeavours. Every developing nation will be owning cube satellites in the coming years. Cubesats can also be hired for a much lower price compared to the bigger ones. Standardisation of satellite systems and miniaturisation of payloads have become a blessing to academia and universities to get into satellite research and studies. Assembling kits of satellites will become cheaper in the coming days. 'Rocketry' is getting more simplified.

5. Offshore Renewable Energy Infrastructure

Cdr (Dr) Jayakrishnan N Nair

Offshore renewable energy installations are increasing across the globe. Finding renewable energy in lieu of fossil fuels has become a big challenge for the global community. The quest for cheap energy has pushed nations to look towards oceans for alternative sources. Global warming is increasing and could severely imbalance the climate in the coming years. Salvaging the wealth from the sea without disrupting the ecosystem could become a game-changer in the coming decade.

"Earth provides enough to satisfy every man's needs, but not every man's greed."

A quote given by the father of our nation, Mahatma Gandhi almost one century ago, quite true for mankind.

Energy from Oceans and Seas

Exploiting the sea by preserving the marine ecosystem is a sustainable recourse for the growth of blue economy. Apart from fish wealth, oceans can be sourced to meet energy requirements for capacity building. Extending these benefits to the remote island nations would help them to actively participate in providing global energy requirement.

Underwater power cable grids can carry a huge capacity of energy across the continents and from the different deep-sea energy sources to land. Offshore High Voltage Direct Current (HVDC) cable grids can be laid across the continents and islands for extending the last mile connectivity.

Let us explore the ways we can tap renewable energy from oceans. Since solar farms and wind farms are very common and have been established for years, let us try to focus on other alternative renewable sources. Cost per unit of power being generated can be worked out to ascertain the economic viability of such projects.

Energy from Sea Waves

The waves are generated continuously over the sea surface. Tapping these waves without disturbing the ecosystem is always a challenge to scientists. ARENA (Australian Renewable Energy Agency) under the Government of Australia has made remarkable progress in this area and are currently steering 14 such projects. European Marine Energy Centre (EMEC) Ltd is another leading organisation that has made great progress in tapping sea-wave energy.

The Wave Energy Converter (WEC) is the key building block for taping this energy. There are many types of technology involved in WEC used for tapping the ocean wave energy, a few of them are given below. Deployment of WEC depends on local sea conditions as well as the maximum sea state during adverse weather conditions. (Fig 5.1)

***Attenuator*:** An attenuator is a floating device that operates parallel to the wave direction and effectively rides the waves. These devices capture energy from the relative motion of the two arms as the wave passes them

***Absorber*:** An attenuator is a floating device that operates parallel to the wave direction and effectively rides the waves. These devices capture energy from the relative motion of the two arms as the wave passes them

***Oscillating Water Column*:** An oscillating water column is a partially submerged, hollow structure. It is open to the sea below the waterline, enclosing a column of air on top of a column of water. Waves cause the water column to rise and fall, which in turn compresses and decompresses the air column. This trapped air is allowed to flow to and from the atmosphere via a turbine, which usually has the ability to rotate regardless of the direction of the airflow. The rotation of the turbine is used to generate electricity.

***Over-Topping*:** 'Over-topping' has a wave lift over a barrier which fills a reservoir with the water and is then drained through a hydro turbine. This technology is very similar to a conventional hydroelectric power dam.

***Inverted-pendulum*:** Oscillating wave surge converters extract energy from wave surges and the movement of water particles within them. The arm oscillates as a pendulum mounted on a pivoted joint in response to the movement of water in the waves. Inverted-Pendulum device uses the motion of waves to move a hinged paddle back and forth. The motion of the paddle drives hydraulic pumps which drive electrical generators.

***Rotating Mass*:** Two forms of rotation are used to capture energy by the movement of the device heaving and swaying in the waves. This motion drives either an eccentric weight or a gyroscope causes precision. In both cases, the movement is attached to an electric generator inside the device.

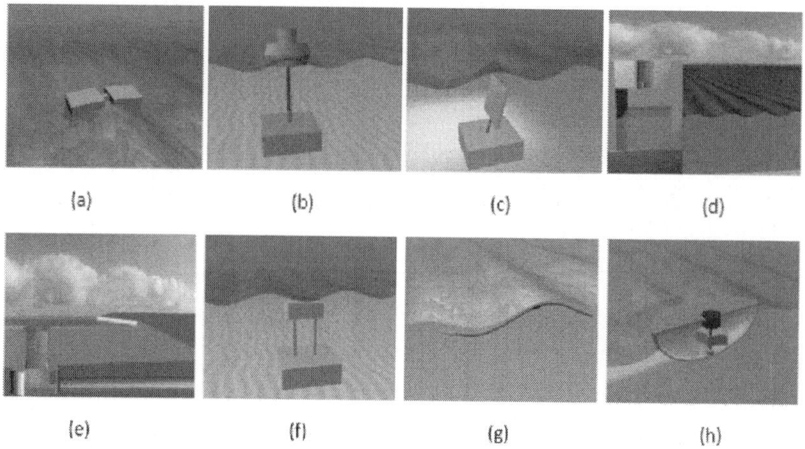

Fig 5.1 (a) attenuator (b) point absorber (c) oscillating wave surge converter (d) oscillating water column (e) over-topping device (f) submerged pressure differential (g) bulge wave (h) rotating mass. PC: Research Gate

Tidal Energy Generation

Tidal energy is renewable energy powered by the natural rise and fall of ocean tides and currents. These technologies include turbines and paddles and are the key element for the generation.

***Horizontal axis turbines*:** Horizontal axis turbines extract energy from moving water in much the same way wind turbines extract energy from moving air. The tidal stream causes the rotors to rotate around the horizontal axis and generate power

***Vertical axis turbines*:** Vertical axis turbines extract energy from the tides in a similar manner mentioned above, however, the turbine is mounted on a vertical axis. The tidal stream causes the rotors to rotate around the vertical axis and generate power.

***Hydrofoil*:** A hydrofoil is attached to an oscillating arm. The tidal current flowing either side of a wing results in lift. This motion then drives fluid in a hydraulic system to be converted into electricity.

Venturi Devices: Venturi Effect devices house the device in a duct that concentrates the tidal flow passing through the turbine. The funnel-like collecting device sits submerged in the tidal current. The flow of water can drive a turbine directly or the induced pressure differential in the system can drive an air turbine.

Archimedes Screw: The Archimedes Screw is a helical corkscrew-shaped device (a helical surface surrounding a central cylindrical shaft). The device draws power from the tidal stream as the water moves up/through the spiral turning the turbines.

Ocean Thermal Energy

Ocean Thermal Energy Conversion (OTEC) is a game-changing technology that leverage the temperature difference in the ocean between cold deep water and warm surface water in the tropics and subtropics to generate unlimited energy. This is ideal for tropical areas/ Indo-Pacific where the temperature difference between deep seawater and surface water is nearing 20 degrees Celsius (Fig 5.3).

Expanding ammonia gas can be used to run the turbine which can be liqucficd at high pressures using cool water from the sea bottom. The conversion of liquid ammonia to gas can be done using warm water at the sea surface. Thus, there are two heat exchangers in each plant. These plants are ideal for remote islands. (Fig 5.3)

Fig 5.2 Tidal Energy Generation PC: The Cool Down

Makai OTEC power plant in the US is the world's biggest operational facility of its kind with an annual power generation capacity of 100kW, which is sufficient to power 120 homes in Hawaii. The plant is connected to the US grid in 2015. Lockheed Martin is further developing and constructing a 10MW OTEC pilot power plant off the coast of southern China in collaboration with Reign-wood Group. There is a huge possibility for island nations located in the tropical Indo-Pacific region to exploit this technology for power generation.

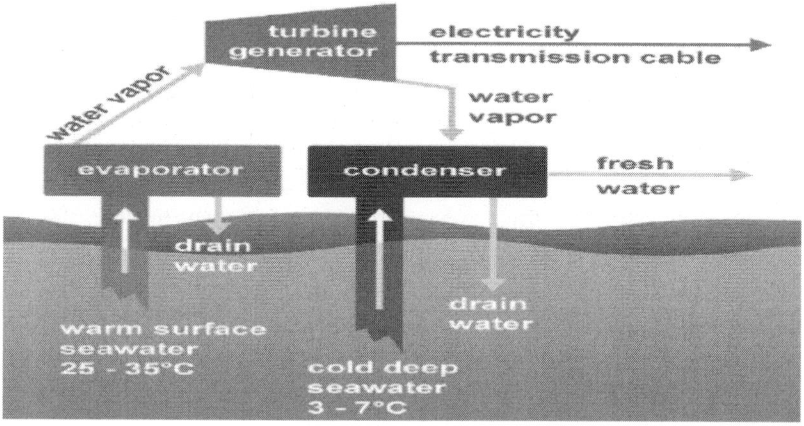

Fig 5.3 OTEC PC: EIA

Energy from Sub Sea Ocean Current

Extracting energy from ocean currents is another difficult task for scientists. Setting up the right turbines underwater is a very cumbersome exercise. Moreover, the ocean currents are at times not predictable. It could change the path. But there are few areas across the ocean where we could get a steady directional current.

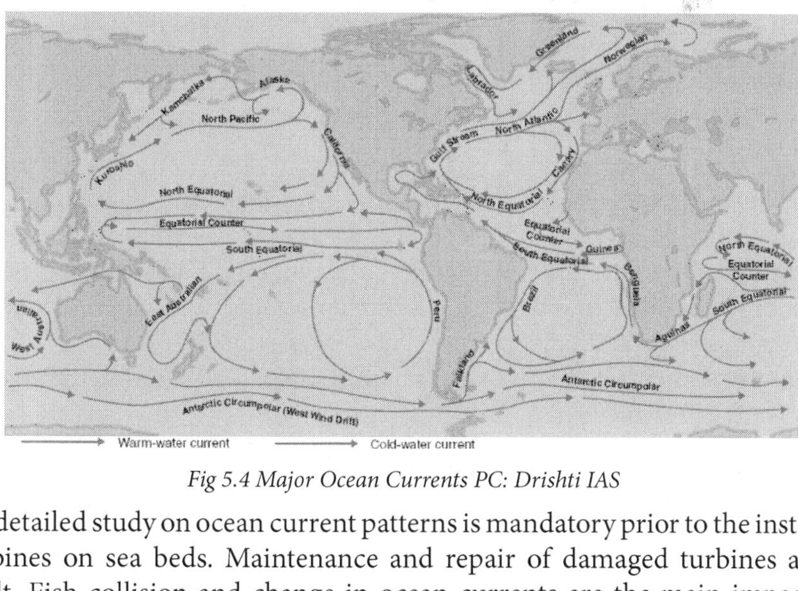

Fig 5.4 Major Ocean Currents PC: Drishti IAS

A detailed study on ocean current patterns is mandatory prior to the installation of turbines on sea beds. Maintenance and repair of damaged turbines are very difficult. Fish collision and change in ocean currents are the main impediments to the generation of energy from ocean current. There are many suitable sites near Vietnam, Japan, Taiwan, and the Philippines having regions with average current speeds reach 1.0–1.4 m per second.

Offshore Geothermal Energy

Only 20 percent of sea beds have been explored by humans so far. There are many unexplored deep-sea ridges, where thermal energy is available and can be exploited. Sea bed surveillance can be done along the mid-ocean ridges across the oceans to find the sources of geothermal energy. Nutrients and energy supplied by vents support communities of deep-sea organisms that are specific to this environment. By recognising these deep-sea ecosystems, we could easily identify the source of geothermal energy (Fig 5.5).

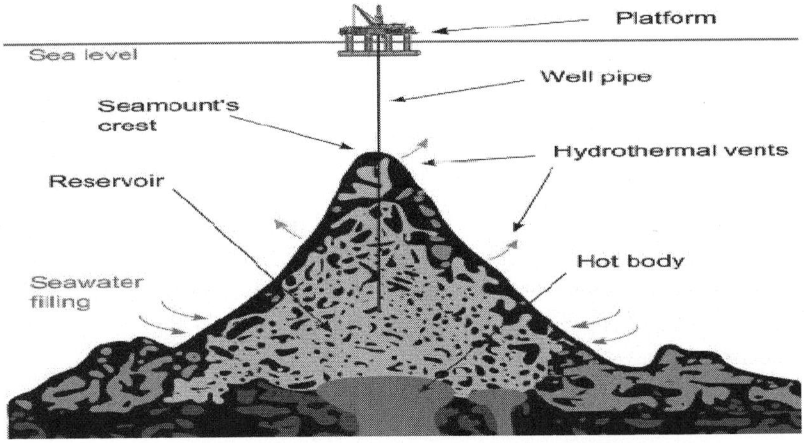

Fig 5.5 Submarine Thermal Vents PC ; Geo energy marketing

A vent is a downward crack in the mid-ocean ridge to depths of 2 to 3 km through the ocean crust where temperature varies from 400–450°C. This super-heated water then re-ascends to the centre of the mid-ocean ridge and emerges as a fast jet at about 350°C. The energy is extracted by pumping cold water to depth using an injection well and then retrieving it at higher temperatures using a production well. At depth, between the wells, water flows through fractures where it is getting heated up. Hot water can be used for generating steam and running turbines.

Floating Solar Farms and Off shore Wind Farms

The solar farm is one of the cheapest and easily implementable solutions on the sea surface. The installation could be undertaken in breakwaters or places where the sea state is low and natural calamities are less. This is very efficient and ideal for tropical sea waters. The disadvantage is that it covers a large area of the sea surface, making it more vulnerable to getting damaged by fishermen folks. Offshore wind farms are the most commonly used renewable source by many nations. Maintenance of these farms has become a little expensive. The associated cables run of wind farms are prone to damage view fishing activities and anchoring.

Deep Sea HVDC Grid

DC power transmission loss is very less compared to the AC transmission loss. Providing an uninterrupted power supply to small islands from renewable sources remains a challenge for the world. A deep-sea worldwide DC current grid is the best solution towards providing power for remote island nations. DC sea-grids can be coupled to shore grids after converting to an AC source. Power stations could be installed along the coastal belt and small islands.

Conclusion

Energy infrastructures are bound to relocate to oceans in the coming decade. The quest for alternative renewable energy sources is driving nations to sea view constraints in getting space over land. A huge percent of our population stays along the coastal belts and hence could become a direct beneficiary from such projects. In future, HVDC ocean grids across continents and islands will become a reality. Floating renewable energy plants may become more common and can become viable for the sustainable growth of our economy.

6. Military Lasers - A Future Market Perspective

Cdr Rupak Berry

Market research brings out future disruptive technologies and how they will impact the existing product portfolio of related companies thereby impacting revenue. Military lasers is a fast-evolving technology and are likely to grow at a very fast pace in the near future. As per the latest research, the military lasers market inclusive of both the Defence and Homeland Security currently stands at almost 4 billion dollars with a Compounded Average Growth Rate (CAGR) of 8.86 %. Military lasers offer certain distinctive features which come with their own pros and cons - but in many application areas, the pros far outweigh the cons thereby making the future look bright for military lasers from a market perspective.

Fig 6.1 Ground Target Destruction PC: New Atlas

Types of Military Lasers

The main types of military lasers are Solid-State Laser, Fiber Laser Chemical Laser, CO2 Laser, and Semiconductor Laser. Of these, Solid State lasers are most widely used. These lasers use batteries and are small in size. They include a diverse product portfolio such as Target Designators, Range finders, Imagers and DIRCMs (Directed Infrared Counter Measures). As per the recent study, Solid-state lasers will grow more in the Asia Pacific and the Middle East in the near future. Market research studies help in identifying favourable technologies which are likely to grow faster thereby helping companies in focusing their growth strategies in that direction. Additionally, they also help in identifying geographies where these technologies would find a better market thereby helping in the most promising geographical expansion.

Product Portfolio

Another area of interest in market research is helping companies in identifying a futuristic product portfolio. For this, it would be important to understand the underlying disruptive technologies which are likely to impact a particular product. In the following paragraphs, few case studies have been enumerated which will bring out these issues. Military Lasers can be used to develop multiple suites of products such as Laser Designators, LIDARs, Laser scanners, Laser Weapons, Laser Range Finders, Ring Laser Gyros, Laser Altimeters, etc. Laser weapons include laser-guided bombs, laser guns, laser dazzlers, etc. It would be of interest for any company to build up a product portfolio that would fetch the best revenues in the future. Traditionally, it has been observed the present revenue mix of any company is likely to change considerably considering future obsolescence of technologies and products both. A few interesting questions that would be addressed by market research would be:

- Which laser products will offer the most lucrative market growth in the next 10 years?
- Which platforms - land, naval or air, are these expected to be deployed the most?
- Why are Ring Laser Gyros showing one of the most prominent markets? Which are the alternative technologies/solutions that may challenge the growth of this segment in the near future?
- What basket of commercial and military laser technology products could be offered to clients?

Military Lasers – Pros & Cons

- **Commercial advantage**: The major advantage of laser weapons over conventional ammunition is the low cost per shot. Each firing of a laser weapon requires only the minimal cost of generating the laser pulse whereas ammunition has to be stored, handled and transported at an additional cost. Lasers can be fired for as little as one dollar per shot, while conventional gun rounds can cost hundreds to thousands of dollars each. However, the developmental cost of laser weapon systems is high. For eg. Cost of a fibre laser weapon system maybe USD 20 million.

- **Flexibility for low and high calibre weapons**: Lasers have an added advantage of scalable power levels allowing them to be used on low-power in a non-lethal mode and high power against more lethal targets such as aircraft and missiles. This is likely to give them an edge to provide a replacement for a large combination of multiple calibre weapons.
- **Simplified Operations**: Lasers do not need any computations unlike for conventional ballistic trajectories for ammunition. They can simply be aimed and re-aimed quickly onto any target and travel at the speed of light.
- **Pain points/Lacunae (Cons):** Lasers are prone to atmospheric absorption, scattering and other losses. Hence, it needs a much higher amount of power to be generated at the source to deliver the required energy to achieve a kill at the target. For eg. It may take 100 MW to be generated at the source to deliver 1 MW required to hit an incoming ballistic missile. Therefore, size and weight may become considerations for deploying lasers, especially on aerial and marine platforms for heavy-duty operations. However, a new technology called adaptive optics, which was developed for telescopes to compensate for atmospheric noise and concentrates the beams aims to overcome some of these challenges.

Military Lasers – A Disruptive Technology

- **For Close-in Weapon Systems (CIWS)**: Considering the present status of tests on laser guns being conducted especially on Naval platforms, a laser weapon could be deployed operationally very soon with an effective range of approximately 1.6 km. This could replace CIWS used to destroy incoming threats in the last mile on Naval as well as other platforms. Companies manufacturing CIWS and other related medium calibre weapons could look at diversifying their product portfolios towards laser weapons in future. The preferred targets for these weapons would be drones, small boats and other similar targets.
- **Non-lethal Applications**: Laser dazzlers come both in the military and

police category to be used in battle and domestic situations. These have been effective in both combat as well as homeland security applications. However, companies have to comply with UN's 1995 Protocol on Blinding Laser Weapons which is the regulatory guideline to be followed in the development of these weapons. Laser dazzlers form 15% of the market in the growing non-lethal laser weapons segment and are offering attractive opportunities to manufacturers. Here, few market research questions could be - Which end-user amongst First Responder, Police Forces and Special Forces is expected to drive this growth? What protocols are inhibiting the growth? A market research perspective covers and answers all.

Contracts and Partnerships

No market research study would be complete without evaluating the emerging contracts and partnerships in the current market scenario. A good market study would empower a client with futuristic insight into entering into contracts/ agreements to get a good head start. For eg., ÉcolePolytechnique and Thales signed a partnership agreement in February 2015 to develop a new revolutionary laser. Now, an analysis shows that France is the major winner of high-tech and photonics contracts, with almost €102 million. French companies awarded contracts include Thales Optronique, Groupe Amplitude, Fastlane, and Alstom.

Conclusion

A future analysis of market potential is imperative for strategic business decision making in any company. Global companies, especially in North America and Europe, are seen to engage market research consultants for both syndicated study as well as consulting assignments. A systematic study of the market in different segments such as technology, type, platforms, application areas, geographies, companies etc goes a long way in providing the much-needed perspective to make a strategic business study complete.

7. Indigenisation-Innovation Architecture-Indian Navy

Dr Vijay Sakhuja

Earlier this month, the Indian Navy put out plans for the twinning of Indigenisation-Innovation and announced setting up of the Naval Innovation and Indigenisation Organisation (NIIO). This initiative is in pursuance of the draft Defence Acquisition Policy 2020 (DAP 20) which mandates the respective armed forces headquarters to set up an 'Innovation & Indigenisation Organisation' in their service. The NIIO builds upon the existing Directorate of Indigenisation of the Indian Navy and would facilitate "end users to interact with academia and industry towards fostering innovation and indigenisation for self-reliance in defence in keeping with the vision of Atmanirbhar Bharat".

One of NIIO's agency i.e. Naval Technology Acceleration Council (N-TAC) "will bring together the twin aspects of innovation and indigenisation and provide apex level directives" and a working group under it will implement the projects. The Technology Development Acceleration Cell (TDAC), under the N-TAC, is specifically meant for "induction of emerging disruptive technology in an accelerated time frame".

Another noteworthy feature of the above architecture is signing of MoUs by the Indian Navy with four agencies i.e. (a) Uttar Pradesh Expressway Industrial Development Authority (UPEIDA), and an official statement quoted Uttar Pradesh Chief Minister Yogi Adityanath saying "With this MOU, the Indian Navy will find solutions of its problems with the help of Centre of Excellence being established in the Defence corridor of UP"; (b) Maker Village, Kochi; (c) the Society of Indian Defence Manufacturers (SIDM); and (d) the Raksha Shakti University (RSU), Gujarat. Professor Bimal Patel, the Director-General of RSU has observed that the MoU with the Indian Navy would trigger "innovations in the security space", augment capabilities of Indian Navy through "incubation assistance to the entrepreneurial start-ups" and the "joint research projects and residential training programs for Indian Navy officers" would be for capacity building of the force. The Maritime Innovation Forum (MIF) of the Security and Scientific-Technical

Research Agency- SASTRA would be spearheaded by the RSU and serve as an "online discussion forum for engaging domestic industry and academic institutes".

'Self-reliance', 'indigenisation' and 'Make in India' have been the mantra of the Indian Navy for over five decades. The Indian Navy has on regular basis issued guideline document such as the 2008 "Indigenisation Plan for the period 2008-2022" which are a reflection of its sophisticated long-term planning. These also showcase its achievements in the 'design and development' of many warships and construction of both conventional and nuclear-propelled submarines in Indian shipyards. The current Indian Navy Indigenisation Plan (INIP) 2015-2030 makes reference to Fourth Industrial Revolution (4IR) technology-enabled systems, devices and platforms and calls for "a need to infuse state-of-the-art technologies in partnership with the Indian industry and prepare our human capital to optimally exploit them to generate maximum combat power".

The Indian Navy's 4IR roadmap is at two levels. First, is the collaborative agreements and arrangement with the laboratories for futuristic technologies under the Defence Research and Development Organisation (DRDO); Council of Scientific and Industrial Research (CSIR); projects through Public Sector Undertakings (PSUs); Indian industry; academia such as the NSTL – Academia Meet on Artificial Intelligence for Naval Systems etc. At the second level, the Indian Navy has set up a 'state-of-the-art' Virtual Reality Centre (VRC) at the Directorate of Naval Design (Surface Ship Group), and under the 'IN – AI Roadmap' it envisages leveraging AI to "enhance the combat edge by imbibing it in operations, maintenance as well as logistics, and further into support verticals, such as physical security, medical diagnostics etc."

While these are impressive initiatives, the Indian Navy must also pursue setting up additional infrastructure to enable it to fully exploit the 4IR technologies that are causing major disruptions in naval affairs across the globe. First, data storage; it is estimated that internet of things (IoT) devices generates 1 billion GB of data every day and by 2025, there would be 42 billion IoT-connected devices globally. This would have to be stored in special storages called Data Centre which would necessarily be physically safe, resistant to seismic activity, flooding, cyber hardened and should be such that these can be expanded. The Data Centre generate enormous amount of heat and require high quality cooling systems and current trends are these are being set up underwater or in the Arctic Circle. The Indian Navy requires secure and robust high-end Naval Data storage infrastructure to enable seamless data-sharing between its organisations and for that it must start examining a suitable site.

Second is about 'test basin' and 'platforms for testing' naval 4IR-enabled prototypes. The government has allocated Rs 400 crore for Defence Testing

Infrastructure Scheme (DTIS) and issued guidelines which "specify the establishment of testing facilities for drones and Unmanned Aerial Vehicles (UAVs), radar, electronics/telecom equipment, rubber testing, noise and shock testing, specialised driving tracks, ship motion testing, ballistics and blast testing, and environmental test facilities." Further, the government plans to set up six to eight test facilities in partnership with private industry in two Defence Industrial Corridors (DICs) one each in Tamil Nadu and Uttar Pradesh. The Indian Navy may require its own specialist test basin; likewise, it would require a "dedicated platform" for testing devices or it may explore to repurpose an existing platform to serve as a Mothership.

For both these requirements, reference can be made to the Andaman & Nicobar (A&N) Islands which have recently been connected with the mainland through an undersea 2,312-kilometre-long optical fibre cable linking Chennai and Port Blair and other places in the north and south islands. This high-speed digital connectivity could help A&N Islands emerge as the optimal destination for testing naval and maritime 4IR enabled platforms for which facilities can be developed jointly under public-private partnership as envisaged under the Defence Testing Infrastructure Scheme (DTIS).

This could even be the beginning of the spawning of the idea of autonomous shipping and smart ports for short sea shipping in the Bay of Bengal connecting Port Blair with Sabang Port, Aceh, Indonesia; Ranong Port, Thailand; and Mongla Port, Bangladesh which has appeared prominently in India's vision of maritime connectivity with ASEAN and BIMSTEC.

Finally, the Naval Innovation and Indigenisation Organisation (NIIO) is a pragmatic initiative and the involvement of academia in the dialogue and engagement with policymakers, Indian Navy, and the industry would help in distinctive policies and boost the development of 4IR technologies, platforms and devices under the Atmanirbhar Bharat initiative.

8. Challenges in Deploying Autonomous Weapon Systems

Cdr (Dr) Jayakrishnan N Nair

Deployment of autonomous weapon systems is going to be a challenging task for nations in the coming years. Artificial Intelligence has pushed the boundaries of autonomy, wherein the human interventions are going to be very minimal in future.

Weapons of Mass destruction (WMD) (Fig 8.1) have been a threat to mankind since World War II. Lethal Autonomous Weapon Systems (LAWS) are posing another kind of threat to humanity. The level of autonomy defines how dangerous the weapon could be for nations. Leading military powers are in a rally to design and develop fully autonomous systems. Human control of machines is minimising since the level of autonomy is increasing year after year. Getting these weapons into the hands of non-state actors is even more dangerous.

Fig 8.1 Autonomous Missile launching PC: Science 2.0

United Nations Institute for Disarmament and Research (UNIDIR) is an autonomous institution under the United Nations which conducts independent research on disarmament and international security issues. They are focused on disarmament and arms control. They engage with the Member States and provide ideas and advice to facilitate dialogue that can advance multilateral arms control and disarmament.

Of late UNIDIR has started focussing on the element of human control over Laws. The decisions are taken at various stages/levels shapes the final outcome of an autonomous engagement. The legal outcome of decisions that a nation can take needs to be deliberated and vetted prior to the implementation of policy governing autonomous systems.

Threat Perception

The underlying threat perceived by a nation from adversaries is a major factor that decides the design of an autonomous system. Stonewalling between nations would lead to generating fear of the unknown between them, triggering the development of systems for self-protection. The perceived threats across borders force the nations and their political leaderships to make decisions which could trigger an autonomous arms race.

Political Decisions

The decisions are taken by the ruling Governments on the development of autonomous weapon systems shape the policy governing them. This decision varies according to the threat perception. The decision taken by the Government is very critical regarding autonomy, which will have ramifications on the strategic and operational decisions. Nations can take decisions on the advancement of autonomous weapon systems to enjoy the geographical/regional hegemony.

Strategic Level Decisions

Once the decisions at the political level are taken on the level of autonomy, the strategic decisions can follow subsequently. The strategy for military operation must comply with Rules of Engagement (ROE) and law including a legitimate military objective which can be successfully achieved through legitimate military means without excessive incidental loss of civilian lives and the collateral damages. A military strategy involves the formulation of specific objectives, including the ways to accomplish objectives. The number of civilian casualties that military action could create with or without seeking approval at the highest/political levels are to be defined. The designated target must be a legitimate military target and must comply with ROE. The law governing should consider the principles of military necessity, distinction, proportionality and precautions. The maturity of political and military leadership will be displayed at this level.

Operational Planning

Strategic-level guidance is translated into operational-level objectives, guidance and intent. These form the cornerstone of the targeting process at the operational and tactical levels. This is a foundational process in identifying the most relevant targets. A target's importance is perceived in its relationship with other targets. Target analysis focuses on identifying these interdependencies and vulnerabilities. After target analysis, target validation, nomination, prioritization and approval is done in this stage. Possible collateral damage also can be worked out. Prepared targets are briefed to the authorized commander, who may consult functional advisers and decide to approve, suspend or disapprove the targets or to forward the decision to the appropriate engagement authority.

Tactical Level Planning

Mission planning is done at the next level. Tactical-level planners perform detailed mission planning for the execution of operations. This may include the location, type, size and material of the target. Planning may include weapon capabilities and effects, civilian patterns of life, time of the attack, munition fragmentation patterns, and secondary explosions. Before deployment, equipment may need to be assessed and modified to comply with applicable requirements and environmental conditions in the battle space.

Mission Execution

At this final critical stage, the target is found, fixed, tracked and engaged. The attack may be ordered, transmitted, monitored and executed. This may include weapons release. The option to suspend or cancel the mission should be available to avoid collateral damage. Post execution, assessments and evaluation are done to measure the effectiveness of the attack for future reference. Achieving a legitimate military objective and proportionality of civilian losses to military advantage is also measured. Assessment should also verify compliance with the rules of engagement viz a viz level of autonomy.

Way Ahead

Deployment of autonomous weapon systems needs detailed in-house deliberations at the apex level in future. The political establishment has a responsible role in defining the level of autonomy of the system being developed. The level of autonomy adopted needs to be under a framework universally accepted by nations. Human elements in the autonomous system should remain and the option to cancel or recall a launched weapon system should be vested with the nation launching the weapons.

We are stepping into another cycle of the cold war. UNIDIR is working overnight to bring all nations to the table to put an end to the ongoing autonomous weapon race. Efforts are to be there to audit the decision-making mechanisms of nations possessing autonomous weapon systems.

9. Laser Dazzlers - Defence and Security Applications

Cdr (Dr) Jayakrishnan N Nair

Laser dazzlers have wide-ranging applications and will soon become a sought-after tool for defence, security and law enforcement agencies.

Recently, Bharat Electronics Limited (BEL) has signed a contract with the Indian Navy towards the supply of 20 laser dazzlers, a non-lethal weapon for warning and stopping suspicious vehicles, vessels, UAV and even aircraft. DRDO has developed this technology and their expertise can be used for domestic manufactures and academia for the design and development of a whole range of dazzler products. We will explore a few applications which can directly aid the defence and security agencies. (Fig 9.1)

First reported use of laser dazzlers was from Royal Navy warships by the British during Falkland's war of 1982. Russians have also used laser dazzlers against Canadian aerial platforms in the straits of Juan de Fuca in April 1997.

The monochromatic characteristics of laser (light amplification by stimulated emission of radiation) give a narrow directive intense beam of non-lethal nature from the laser gun, which could be used against the suspects/ enemy for varied purposes.

Besides military-specific applications, dazzlers are also used by law enforcement agencies to control the riot, mob, to carry out counter-insurgency operations and to protect critical assets in the industry.

Laser dazzlers are capable of blinding the personnel by glare from laser beams. Even optical sensors/ receivers of UAV and aircraft can be incapacitated. The rays could disorient, confuse or even blind a person temporarily. Most devices are configured with Nd-YAG (neodymium-doped yttrium aluminium garnet) modules operating at wavelength 532 nanometre and are designed to produce power density in the range of 0.2 – 0.6 milliwatts/sq cm at the target plane.

There is a huge opportunity for the domestic industry in the coming decade for designing and developing dazzlers for varied applications in the defence and security sector. Few applications are given below.

Fig 9.1 DRDO Laser Gun PC: ADDA247

Protection of Critical Infrastructures from Aerial Threats

Laser-guided Precision Guided Munitions (PGM) are smart weapons/ smart munitions, laser-guided, intended to hit precisely a specific target, to minimize collateral damage and increase lethality against intended targets. Laser dazzlers can be used to misguide these approaching weapons away from the high-value targets. The long-range laser dazzler systems mounted on Gimbal platforms are equipped with the electro-optic tracker integrated to a network of radars would provide 24×7 protection to strategic assets from airspace violation by aerial platforms. Majority of aircraft launched weapon systems are now being guided with laser technology. The critical ground assets are very vulnerable to airborne attacks aided with laser-guided weapons. By installing dazzlers around such critical installation would certainly protect the high-value asset from laser-guided weapons reaching them. The system acts as an Electronic Counter Measure against approaching laser-guided munitions.

Protection of Military Aircraft from Ground-Based Laser Guided Weapons

The Self Protection System (SPS) is one of the most critical systems on board military aircraft, which will protect aircraft from the approaching laser-guided weapons including shoulder-launched infrared-guided missiles. Laser dazzlers designed for this specific purpose can misguide the approaching missiles/ rockets launched from the ground and protect the aircraft from disaster by blanking the receiver of approaching anti-aircraft missile system.

As a Gun mount for Illuminating and Designating Targets

Subject technology can also be used for illuminating the target being tracked prior to firing. The axis of the dazzler mounted laser gun to be designed parallel with the axis of the muzzle of the gun barrel. This gives much-required accuracy for soldiers in combat. This can be used as a non-lethal way to check the enemy soldiers and targets by pointing at them.

Clutter Free WiFi (Li-Fi) Communication

Mode of transmission plays a significant role in wifi communication systems. Light/laser as a mode of communication with added encryption makes the data/information more secure than the existing radio waves. This mode of communication termed Li-Fi is ideal for cluttered environments. Dedicated optical transmitter-receivers can be used for using laser dazzler communication and data transmission.

Underwater Communication

Underwater water communication is always a big challenge for Indian naval submarine arm. Sound does have limitations since the water as a medium has varied density across the globe. The blue-green laser is a potential candidate for high bandwidth underwater wireless communication because of its high data transfer rate, reasonably large range, small size, low power consumption, immunity to interference and jamming and covertness of transmission. 450 nm wavelength. InGaN laser diode laser is an ideal solution for underwater communication. It is possible to reach data rates up to 9 Gbit/secs speed underwater.

Search and Rescue (SAR) at Sea

The wide expanse of sea and ocean currents pose a greater challenge for the Navy while undertaking the search and rescue missions. Spotting the distress/debris at sea is the first step in the SAR at sea. Long-range laser dazzlers integrated with a 360° gimbal base and an electro-optic tracker can be mounted on rescue ships and deck choppers to speed up the process of rescue at sea.

Guiding Weapons to Target

As a target designator, dazzlers are very effective in guiding airborne and ground-based weapons to target. The homing system encapsulated inside the nose cone of the weapon can guide the munition to the designated target. Dazzler system laser signal frequency can be designed in accordance with that of the laser munition.

Riot and Mob Control

Dazzlers can be used as an aid for law enforcement agencies to confuse the rioting mob at gunpoint without harming them. Laser dazzler systems with day/night time operational ranges of the order of 250 – 500 meters can be used for this purpose. The system has immense potential in our country and would provide much-needed support in anti-terrorist operations. A vehicle mount system has already been developed by DRDO in the year 2019.

Countering Bird Menace at Airfields

Bird activities remain as a major hurdle for fighter operations across the subcontinent. A bird hit could write off an aircraft from the inventory and could become detrimental for the Airforce in forwarding areas while operations. Dazzlers can scare and keep birds away from the aircraft flying zones and make it safe for fighters and other military aircraft to land and take-off incident-free. An array of lasers can create a light fence to restrict bird activity along with glide slopes of airfields.

For Killing Enemy Satellites

Russians have developed aircraft mount dazzlers (high energy dazzler) to track and kill enemy low flying satellites. Russia has an existing laser weapons program, specifically targeting satellites, and that program builds off similar Soviet-era efforts such as the Beriev-A-60 gas laser and Kontakt 30P6 programs, which could be used to disrupt satellites or bring them down. Russian defence manufacturer M/s Almaz-Antey has completed this anti-satellite complex project with laser, radar, and ground elements and has proved this system from a new airborne platform.

Satellite-Based Membrane Reflector Balloon for Illuminating OTH Targets

Satellite-based membrane reflector balloon is currently in the developmental stage. These are laser dazzlers with global coverage. The system has a remote-controlled satellite mounted with membrane reflector for receiving the dazzling laser beam from the source station placed at the earth and could illuminate target location and expose them to laser-guided munitions.

Conclusion

A variety of laser dazzler gadgets are likely to enter the market in the coming decades. A modular approach could be used for designing and developing dazzler guns to facilitate plugin across various platforms. Handheld and weapon-mounted laser dazzlers could have a worldwide market and can be manufactured and exported in the coming years. Since DRDO has done remarkable progress in this area, our academia, industry and startups can collaborate with DRDO for further research, ideation and enhancement.

10. Hypersonic Program of India: Hype or Rewarding

Cdr Sandeep Dhawan

In September 2020, Defence Research and Development Organisation (DRDO) tested its Hypersonic Technology Demonstration Vehicle or HSTDV. During the test, the HSTDV attained a speed of Mach 6 for 23 seconds. Hurrah, India, had crossed a milestone and joined the elite club of nations with such a technology.

Today there is a race between nations to develop and demonstrate their hypersonic weapons to the world as if their life depends upon them. Is that true? We can't fight a modern war without these weapons, or should hypersonic weapons be treated just like any other weapon?

Hypersonic Weapon Systems

Hypersonic is a term used to describe any platform that can travel at speeds in excess of Mach 5 or 6174 kilometres per hour. Are those speeds unique? Not really. Modern missiles have reached hypersonic speeds since the days of Hitler's V-2 rockets. In fact, the American design of the 70s, Minuteman III, Inter Continental Ballistic Missiles (ICBMs) achieve speeds in excess of Mach 23, and India's Agni-5 reaches Mach 24.

Therefore, the whole hype about modern hypersonic weapons is not just about extreme speeds. It is the combination of manoeuvrability, extreme speed, and unpredictable trajectory, without revealing their target until the last moment, making them all alluring and difficult to intercept (Fig 10.1). Hypersonic weapons in the fray are:

- **Hypersonic Boost Glide Vehicles (HGVs):** These are like traditional long-range ballistic missiles. High-velocity boosters take these vehicles to the upper atmosphere. Then they glide towards their target unpowered. China's Dongfeng-17 (DZ-ZF), Russia's Avangard, and the U.S. Navy's Conventional Prompt Strike Systems are some examples.
- **Hypersonic Aero-ballistic System:** It is dropped from an aircraft,

accelerated to hypersonic speed using a rocket, and then follows a ballistic, meaning unpowered, trajectory. The Russian Kinzhal system used in Ukraine is one such example.

- **Hypersonic Cruise Missiles**: These use a scramjet propulsion system and act more like hypersonic aircraft. India's BrahMos-2, Russia's Tsirkon (NATO SS-N-33), and the U.S. Hypersonic Air-breathing Weapon Concept (HAWC) are some of the existing concepts.

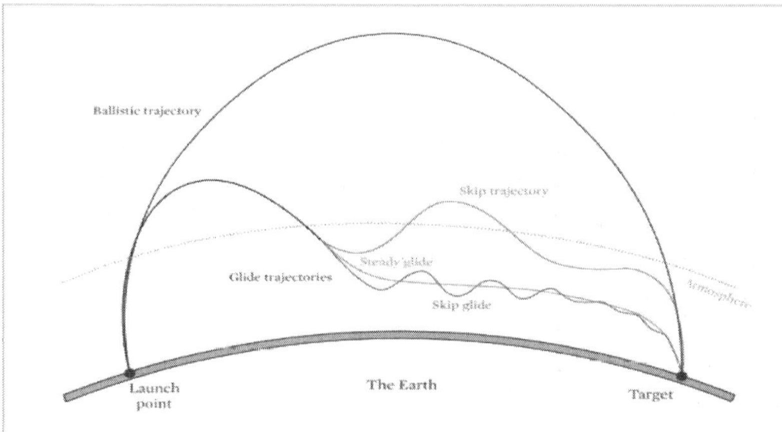

Fig 10.1 Types of Trajectories PC: SIPRI

Capabilities

There is no doubt that hypersonic weapons present an element of surprise and compress the response time within the Observe–Orient–Decide–Act loop. It is also clear that modern anti-missile systems are not capable of intercepting hypersonic vehicles. At least, that's how their invincibility is usually advertised to the public. But the biggest question is — do they live up to the hype, and are they worth it?

Just like India, Russia and China have also tested hypersonic boost-glide weapons, the Avangard and DZ-ZF, respectively. India and Russia joint venture is also working on a hypersonic BrahMos platform. However, no nation has managed to field an operational hypersonic cruise missile to date. The United States claims to have tested Hypersonic Air-breathing Weapon Concept (HAWC) in March 2022. But nothing concrete has emerged out of it. So that leaves us with only the glide vehicles.

HGVs have some uphill engineering challenges that will require a hell of a lot of money to overcome, and despite that, some physical limitations will never be overcome. Therefore, hypersonic weapons can't do A, B, and C tasks. Instead, it is more precise to declare that HGVs can do A or B, or C tasks.

What are those issues? Let us analyze them one by one. The first issue is energy and speed. The gliders lose power and resultant loss of speed soon after the boost part is over. As they accelerate down to their target, they carry out manoeuvres. These manoeuvres result in increased drag, which mandates additional thrust to maintain speed. Even a scramjet engine cannot compensate for this induced drag. HGVs, in any way, don't have an engine. The more they manoeuvre, the more induced drag is produced, further lowering the actual speed of impact. This could certainly reduce the speed below Mach 5. This is a significant limitation. Now imagine the effect of manoeuvrability on the missile's kinetic energy impact at intercontinental ranges.

Hypersonic weapons are slaves of extreme speed. The adverse effect of high speed is friction. The friction produces heat. The surface temperature of hypersonic vehicles exceeds 2,000°C. This would produce a line of ionized gas that could disrupt navigation signals, impacting accuracy. Even ICBMs have a circular error probable of 120 m. The HGV itself could avoid the detection, but the trail of the plasma would be visible on radars, space-based sensors, and even to large surveillance drones, and that is a very big giveaway. Therefore, though the glider itself would deceive the detection systems, the low-altitude atmospheric flights expose hypersonic weapons hiding from surface-based radars behind the Earth's curvature.

The cost of hypersonic vehicles is another big dampener. A Pentagon estimate suggested the United States Air Force HGVs may cost as much as $106 million apiece. Now maybe the Indian HGV might cost much lesser than the American one, but still, there is no comparison. An extended-range supersonic BrahMos missile costs $4.85 million. The Agni-5 ICBM will likely cost $6-8 million apiece. That means Indian forces could buy over 15 to 20 highly capable missiles in the budget of a hypersonic weapon. They can even buy a modern 4.5-generation fighter jet for the same amount, serving them for a couple of decades.

In April 2018, the U.S., U.K., and France fired 105 subsonic Tomahawk cruise missiles at targets in Syria. They also reported that the Syrian forces fired more than 40 interceptors at the inbound missiles without successfully destroying a single missile. Russia countered the news by stating they had intercepted more than 70 inbound missiles. Let us assume both sides are telling lies & the Syrian forces were able to destroy 50 percent of the missiles. Even then, it leaves us with huge numbers of missiles to overwhelm any radar system. Now Tomahawk costs just $2 million apiece. That means for the cost of one hypersonic weapon; allies could fire 50 subsonic cruise missiles.

Now don't get me wrong. Hypersonic weapons are an outstanding achievement for any country and an engineering and scientific marvel. Harnessing such a technology demonstrates the technological prowess of a nation. However, one has to look at the usage of HGVs dispassionately. Why are the Russian hypersonic weapons not raining down on sensitive Ukrainian sites to make the victory quicker? The reason is simple, as we have discussed. They are prohibitively expensive, have engineering limitations, and are still in the evolutionary stage. (Table 10. 1 refers)

Evolutionary or Revolutionary

Table 10.1 Information Courtesy: SIPRI

Designator/ programme	Type	Booster/propulsion	Payload	Range (km)	Status	MTCR Partner
Australia and United States						*Yes*
SCIFiRE (prog.)	HCM	Scramjet engine and rocket booster	Conventional	..	Under development since 2021; speed of Mach>5; builds on HIFiRE prog.	
China						*No*
DF-ZF	HGV	..	..	(Inter-continental range)	First flight tested in 2014	
DF-17	HGV	DF-16 ballistic missile booster	(dual-capable)	1 600–2 400	Deployed since 2019; last flight-tested in 2017	
..	HGV	Fractional orbital bombardment system	..	Global range	First flight-tested in Aug. 2021	
Starry Sky-2	HCM	Air-breathing engine	Nuclear	..	Experimental system; flight-tested in 2018	
North Korea						*No*
Hwasong-8	HGV	Boost-glide system; ground-launched; road-mobile	(nuclear or dual-capable)	..	First flight-tested in Sep. 2021	
..	Aero-ballistic	Boost-glide system; ground-launched; road-mobile	(nuclear or dual-capable)	..	First flight-tested in Jan. 2022	
France						*Yes*
ASN4G	HCM	Air-breathing engine; air-launched	Nuclear	..	Under development	
V-MAX (prog.)	HGV	Boost-glide system	(nuclear)	..	Under development	
India						*Yes*
HSTDV (prog.)	HCM	Air-breathing engine; Agni-1 missile booster	..	..	Demonstrator tested in 2019	

Most commanders consider hypersonic weapons to be more tactical than strategic. However, the October 2021 Chinese Fractional Orbital Bombardment

System (FOBS) changed the game. The hypersonic glide vehicle carrying the warhead stayed in low-earth orbit, circled the globe, reentered the atmosphere, and attacked its target. The warhead missed its target by 25 kilometres, but this was no mean achievement. Today China is far ahead of the United States, Russia and India in developing such capabilities.

Way Ahead

Xi'an is a large city and capital of Shaanxi Province in central China. It is about 1400 km from India's North East. A Nirbhay missile with an average speed of Mach .8 would take approximately 1 hour and 25 minutes to hit the city. An HGV travelling at Mach 10 would cover the same distance in under seven minutes. It demonstrates that an HGV launched from 1200 km gives the same reaction time as a subsonic cruise missile launched from 100 km.

India has taken a few baby steps in the evolution of hypersonic weapons. India needs to double down the road for a simple reason, and it is not Clausewitzian capability; instead, it is a Sun Tzu-inspired strategy, i.e., to win without fighting. Tomorrow's hypersonic weapons would be utilized not to fight but to give improved deterrence capability to avoid a war.

Even the Chinese would be in a dilemma when using any such weapon against India. India should clarify that the launch of dual capability (conventional or nuclear) Chinese ICBM DF-41 against an Indian target would be assumed to be a nuclear attack. The tactical hypersonic weapon Starry Sky-2 (Xing Kong-2) used against Indian aircraft carriers would also be considered a nuclear attack. Therefore, India would retaliate, escalating the war into a nuclear one.

As I write, China is busy transferring many conventional platforms like Type 054A/P frigates, Type-039B submarines, J-10C fighters, and their repair facilities to Pakistan for obvious reasons. However, as of now, there is no need for them to transfer the hypersonic weapons to Pakistani soil because they work very well from the Chinese territory, covering all of the Indian territories.

To sum it up, hypersonic weapons alone cannot resolve India's security dilemma. At the same time, Indian agencies cannot take their own sweet development time as if it is the 70s. Rather hypersonic weapons have to be developed at double speed and utilized along with other new technologies like cyber activities, advanced submarine warfare, and space operations, as well as conventional fighting forces to win future wars.

11. Wearable for Soldiers

Cdr (Dr) Jayakrishnan N Nair

Wearable are revolutionary products that could impact our armed forces in the coming years. Napoleon Bonaparte quotes "To have good soldiers, a nation must always be at war." This quote is germane, but do we care for the survival of our soldiers? Well, wearable can do it for us. Many equipment and gadgets can become an integral part of a soldier's wearable or his uniform, making him free from carrying additional payloads.

Wired soldiers (Fig 11.1) mounted with a series of microsensors can be integrated to a wireless captive network and to a cloud-based centralised server. Dedicated applications can be developed to monitor and control the soldiers deployed in hazardous missions by 'Digitally Twinning' them. We can create 'Net Warriors' in future with Wireless Body Area Networks (WBANs).

Fig 11.1 Wearables -Soldier PC:Research gate

Remarkable progress has been made in the sports and medical fields with the support of wearables. Armed forces are yet to exploit this technology for the comfort of soldiers. Wearables can be tailored suiting to the specific requirements of soldiers.

An article on 'smart couture for soldiers' was published at Defence Research and Study platform by Dr Vijay Sakujha a few days back. Today we will focus on other areas of applications. The military wearables market is projected to grow from USD 4.2 billion in 2019 to USD 6.4 billion by 2025, at a CAGR of 7.2% from 2019 to 2025.

Infrastructure

Building network infrastructure along the border is a very important stride in bringing wearables to soldiers. Establishing a reliable backbone fibre connectivity is an absolute requirement for keeping soldiers connected. These fibre networks can be terminated with wireless networks similar to 4G/5G for establishing the last mile connectivity. India has given great impetus for the up-gradation of road infrastructure along borders in the last few years. Communication networks can be the next in line. Implantable sensor technology includes technology like Wireless Body Area Networks (WBANs) coupled with technologies like the Internet of Battlefield Things (IoBT) would make battlefield management fully digital. A Multi-Level Fusion Framework (MLFF) based on Body Sensor Networks (BSNs) of soldiers would make a unique heterogeneous sensor network model.

Biometric Sensors

Development of miniature sensors for biometric applications has opened expansive opportunities. Sensors can even be implanted under the skin for specific needs. Powering sensors and getting appropriate voltage proportional to the varying parameters of the human body is a difficult exercise. Sensors are charge-coupled devices or CMOS image sensors. Textile sensors can be designed to measure temperature, biopotential for cardiogram, myographs, encephalography, acoustic signals for diagnosing heart, lungs, digestion, and joints. Ultrasound can be used for blood flow, motion for respiration, pressure for BP, radiation for IR, spectroscopy as well as odour and sweat for skin parameters.

Applications

Many wrists worn wearable devices are currently available in the market from Fitbits, Garmins, Apple, and Samsung as well as strap-based devices from Polar and Garmin products, besides high-end devices from Zephyr and Hidalgo Equivital.

Our soldiers undertake many hazardous missions on a daily basis. They are deployed at hostile and remote areas, where their mental and health conditions are always tested for survivability. In this information era, we should explore and identify how we can wire our soldiers and put them at a comfort level during their missions. Few established applications are given below.

Health Monitoring

'More you sweat in the peacetime, less you bleed in war'. This is very true, but it does not imply that we should keep our warriors unsafe while on a mission. The success story of warriors on missions is directly linked to the mental and physical well-being. A range of sensors integrated into the soldier's body can monitor the soldier's health in real-time. The biometric sensors integrated to clothing can sense vitals such as heart rate, respiratory rate, ECG, EEG oxygen level, body temperature etc. Army men at high altitudes, navy commandos deployed for underwater missions and fighter pilots under G load can be connected up and monitored during the mission to keep them safe. Even predictive analysis can be done on their vital data to avoid disaster using Artificial Intelligence.

Performance Monitoring

Training is an incessant activity in the armed forces. Soldiers and men in uniform are engaged in training activity for more duration during peacetime. The threshold level of every warrior is tested and ascertained during the training. Performance monitoring can be gauged during the training/simulation phase for many activities. This performance data would certainly help in selecting and nominating men for specific missions. The biometric sensors can sense and monitor muscle activity, muscle fatigue, muscle symmetry, speed, acceleration levels, and distance travelled, blood flow to the brain.

Warming Jacket

Outdoor missions remain a challenge for soldiers in winter and at high altitudes. The temperature can be automatically controlled/regulated at the optimum level through wired costumes which could keep the soldiers comfortable. Providing these jackets to soldiers would save a large amount of energy compared to bunker/room heating.

Tagging Soldiers

Radio Frequency Identification (RFID) tagging is one of the most popular applications in the military environment. Planting a microchip under the skin with an RFID detection technology may be an option to tag the soldiers. Identification chips can be made as a part of the wearable device and can be used for monitoring the movement of soldiers in a tactical area, ships and even inside submarines. This could disrupt the fingerprint biometric system.

Infra-red (IR) Shielding Uniform

IR and thermal stealth uniforms can effectively block IR and thermal radiation emitted from the human body. The material used for this shield uses a polyurethane–antimony tin oxide (PU–ATO) composite fibre. By wearing this shield/ uniform, the soldiers will remain stealth from IR and thermal cameras. This will provide added security for soldiers during night operations.

Conductive Textile

Conductive textiles can be either made by depositing conductive layers onto non-conductive textiles or using conductive fibres. Textiles can be a part of electronic component circuitry that create systems capable of sensing, heating, lighting or transmitting data. Electronics flushed on textile fabrics can sense, compute, communicate, and actuate. Electronic equipment being carried for missions can become an integral part of wearables/ uniforms.

Battery Charging

Power management is a very critical factor for missions. If footwear/boots can convert the pressure of heels to electrical energy, this energy can be used to power equipment and batteries integrated with soldiers. Sole of the shoe is connected to a power pack fitted outside the shoe and collects kinetic energy using a gear mechanism that converts linear motion generated while walking into rotational motion which would spin a generator which charges the battery continuously. This will be very useful for foot soldiers under patrolling duties along the border.

Printed Antenna

Carrying a communication device antenna is always a painful activity for foot soldiers. Textile antennas are a special class of antennas that are partially or entirely made out of textile materials, unlike conventional antennas which have rigid materials. The textile antennas have electrically conductive fabrics with radiating and grounding parts and also have dielectric materials for the insulation. These smart textile systems can facilitate body-centric communication between tower and soldiers as well as a soldier to soldier.

Medical Curing Wearables

Movement of casualty during an evacuation should be made safe and there is a need to move in specially designed warming and IR radiating suits while evacuation to keep the body parts safe and healing. This is purely a medical application

Helmet Mount Display System (HMDS)

HMDS which improves situational awareness with icons and graphics that are visible within the user's Field of View (FOV) like what pilots have while flying fighter aircraft. The Net Warrior (NW) can see-through a helmet-mounted display in limited visibility. Even target acquisition with bore-sighted weapon sight imagery can be integrated into the soldier's FOV. The device can be designed with voice activation using a boom microphone. Even augmented reality can be integrated into the display system. AI can be facilitated generating predictive data on display aiding soldiers for making decisions.

Helmet Mount Cameras

Helmet mount cameras can be of IR or Night Vision enabled to get a clear vision during night operations. A reverse looking camera across the face can be mounted to view the face of the networked soldier from a remote location. The miniaturisation of components associated with camera technology has certainly helped mounting lightweight gadgets to helmets. A rear looking camera coupled to Helmet Mount Display could become a lifesaver for soldiers.

Communication and Navigation

Blockchain based secure communication systems with every soldier can be deployed as an added layer of security along with crypto. The current smart watches integrated with functions currently available in our smart phones with wireless technology similar to 4G/5G communication infrastructure can help the soldiers remain connected from their base station while navigating. Many sensors can be integrated into such wearable devices for centralised monitoring and control.

Way Ahead

There is a need to improve the comfort level and safety of soldiers deployed for missions. It is absolutely necessary that they remain connected and wired for their safety. The human factor of wearable technology needs to be considered by developers by understanding the needs and comfort level of users. Developers must realise that the system that they are contributing could save the lives of soldiers and would have a positive impact on men in combat. There is a huge opportunity for academia and incubators to explore wearable technologies and bring in new ideas for implementation.

12. Drone Attacks - 12 ways to Defend

Cdr (Dr) Jayakrishnan N Nair

The drone is becoming more relevant for military applications view autonomous features and stealthy characteristics.

"When people don't respect one another, seldom is there honesty", Shannon L Alder quotes. So be the warfare in future. Rules and ethics are seldom followed and there will be always surprises from the enemy side.

Revolution in Military Affairs (RMA) is inevitable and future warfare is married to disruptive technologies in this information era. Autonomy and decision making based on AI and MI would change the existing conventional war to algorithmic warfare. The nations having a traditional ground force could be debilitated overnight by unconventional weapons and disruptive tactics. The only alternative available to survive is to disrupt the disruptor.

The rotary-wing drones are no more toys. They are silent and are capable of flying low and remain stealth during the flight. Detecting them is a big challenge over the uneven terrain. The manufacturing cost of these birds is very less, ideal for all the suicidal missions. Since one of our neighbours is the leading manufacturer of these kinds of drones, it is essential for us to gear up and not to wait for a disaster to learn. Recently concluded conflict between Armenia and Azerbaijan gave us some critical inputs.

Swarms of hundreds of drones with precision-guided explosives can choke our radars and demolish the frontline defence. They can increase war-zone vulnerability by lighting up air, ground or sea targets for shadowing missiles and fighter aircraft. New age drones with less human intervention can be programmed to go deep into well-defended territories with reduced risk attached.

There is an immediate requirement to institute and deploy effective counter-drone mechanisms along the borders to effectively tackle this menace. In this article, we will explore the ways and means to counter-drone attacks. Our focus will be exploring anti-drone technologies for micro and small drones (less than 25 kg) both fixed and rotary wing.

Anti-Drone Technologies - Detection, Defending and Destroying

Anti-drone systems comprise detection, interception and eventually neutralising unwanted UAVs/Drones (Fig 12.1). The process can eventually terminate the enemy drones mid-air. There are many ways we could accomplish these tasks.

Fig 12. 1 Defending Drones PC: Military.com

Radar

Frequency Modulated Continuous Wave (FMCW) AESA radar is the most suitable candidate for counter-drone operations. Providing a 180° Azimuth by 85° elevation antenna array could cover a large area of detection. It can send out signals and receives the echoes for measuring direction and distance. It can be engaged for constant tracking, can handle hundreds of targets simultaneously and can be operated day night in all weather conditions. It can be set to autonomous mode and we can generate quick alerts/alarms on detection of drones.

Electromagnetic Wave Receivers

This system looks for Electromagnetic signals being emitted by the UAV/drone and detects the location of drones using triangulation. The system functions similar to ESM systems. This is fairly accurate and can do detection of targets much better than the radars. An array of receivers can be deployed along the borders to detect the approaching drones

Audio Sensors

Usually, a microphone or microphone array could detect the sound made by a drone and calculate the direction. More sets of microphones can be used for triangulation and fixing positions of approaching drones. Though it is very cost-effective, ambient noises can play spoilsport. This is an ideal choice for very short ranges up to 500 meters.

Optical Sensors

These are essentially video cameras with telescopic characteristics and high-resolution optical sensors. Besides daylight capabilities, it can have infrared or thermal imaging for night operations. It could provide visuals of drones and it's payload and can record images. It has the disadvantage of high false-alarm and poor performance in adverse weather conditions/ dark.

Dronegun/ Radio Frequency Jammer

The drone gun sends jamming frequencies that choke the communication and control signals between the drone controller and the flying drone. The system breaks the link between the drone and it's pilot, thereby forcing them to head back home or land where it is. It is a rifle shaped device that uses radiofrequency jamming and GPS jamming to counter drones. It can have coverage up to 1 km in a wide range environment condition. RF Jammer can also be a static transmitter which transmits a large amount of RF energy towards the drone, masking the controller signal.

Electronic Fence

An electronic fence is an Electronic Counter Measures (ECM) system which prevents drones from flying into a defended location. It can be configured horizontally or vertically depending on the terrain requirements. This is programmable and can be stimulated via an array of sensors. Skyfence antennas are fixed along the border as a fence and it generates an electromagnetic wave 'wall' extending into the sky up to 500 meters in height. The secondary field ensures that there are no gaps in the system. Sensors could jam the drone's computer and block its frequency and control protocols and divert it back to where it came from.

GPS Spoofer

Spoofer misguides the drone by sending counterfeit codes and GPS signals to the drone corrupting the navigation data of the drone. The spoofer is implemented on a portable software-defined radio platform with a digital signal processor (DSP) at its core. This platform comprises radio frequency (RF) front-end that down-mixes and digitizes GPS L1 and L2 frequencies. A DSP board that performs acquisition and tracking of GPS L1 C/A, calculates a navigation solution, predicts the L1 C/A data bits, and produces a consistent set of spoofed GPS L1 C/A signals which misguides the drone to destruction.

Hackers

Hackers take control of enemy drones and drift them to a safe place for landing or for further investigation or neutralisation. This is done by overriding the existing control. Drones can be recovered later or even destroyed.

High Energy Laser

A high-powered optical device which produces an extremely focused beam of light, or a laser beam. The radio spectrum of a drone is very narrow, so a focused broadcast is enough to bring down the drone. The laser defeats the drone by destroying the structure and/or the electronics. This will physically incapacitate the drone. It is a costly solution which can create collateral damage during the operation.

High Energy Microwave

High Power Microwave (HPM) devices generate an Electromagnetic Pulse (EMP) capable of disrupting electronic devices. The EMP interferes with radio links and disrupts or even destroys the electronic circuitry in drones. HPM devices may include an antenna to focus the EMP in a certain direction, reducing potential collateral damage. The drone can be stopped effectively in a non-kinetic mode. This is a high-cost solution which could even disrupt communications or destroy other electronic devices in the area of operation.

Drone Catcher

Drone catcher is a net gun-armed multi-copter which safely eliminates illegal drones from the air. With the help of multiple onboard sensors, the net gun locks on the target and then shoots a net to catch the drone target. After the catch, the drone catcher carries the captured drone on a cable to a harmless place and releases it. If the caught drone is too heavy to be carried, it drops it with the help parachute to ensure a low impact on the ground. Firing a net at a drone, or otherwise bringing a net into contact with a drone stops the drone by prohibiting the rotor blades.

Trained Attack Birds

Though not a polished way to do, it can be done with the support of bird lovers by effective training. We should avoid this for drones with detonators, which could be suicidal for the birds deployed.

Way Ahead

Let us accept the fact that conventional warfare is facing disruption. Days are not far where weapon-mounted drones may become buddies for the foot soldiers.

Integration of multi-layer anti-drone mechanisms could build up a foolproof drone defence infrastructure along the borders. Academia and Incubators can certainly focus their research in this area in the coming months to help our industry and armed forces.

Sky fencing would guarantee a foolproof detection against drone intrusion. More field study needs to be carried out in uneven terrains to beat the stealthy characteristics of drones. Low flying drones are very difficult to detect and neutralise. There is a need to recalibrate our front-line deployment strategy along the border.

13. Military Drones-15 New Found Applications

Cdr (Dr) Jayakrishnan N Nair

"Brutality and injustice made us raise our hands towards the sky for years, God didn't respond to us, but drones came to our rescue." **M.F. Moonzajer**

Smart phones have revolutionised our lives in the past decade. Drones are the next which could impact our lives in the coming decade. The Armed Forces cannot endure in isolation and will be a major market for military drones in the coming years. The quote above is also applicable to the military. As a nation, we are still far from exploring the possibilities of drones in military applications. Albeit UAVs being a part of our military operations, they are yet to go beyond surveillance and weapon delivery applications. We can tour the varied possibilities which could aid the armed forces in years to come. An advanced version of UCAV of DAPRA (Fig 13.1) can be as effective as fighter being stealthy.

Fig 13.1 DAPRA UCAV PC:Eurasia Review

Changing Role of Drones

Miniature pilot less aircraft or flying mini robots, drones are rapidly growing in popularity. The Two-week-long Nagorno-Karabakh conflict between Azerbaijan and Armenia has given some indications on the lethality of cheap low flying stealth drones. This war also showed us some indications on the vulnerability of tanks and artillery vehicles in the years to come. Are drones going to disrupt the way of fighting the conventional war?

It is now apparent that airborne disposable autonomous drones are more lethal than land-based robots and autonomous ground vehicles. In pursuit of designing and developing smaller and lighter subsystems, platforms based on MEMS and nanotechnology opened a large area of innovative disruptive technology in the area of military drones. There is an urgent need to equip our force and to reinvent our tactics in the wake of recent developments at Nagorno-Karabakh since the neighbour at our eastern border is capable of springing a similar surprise.

Autonomy

The level of autonomy of military drones is increasing every year. Autonomous military drones blended with artificial intelligence being developed are stealthy, have sensor fusion, various channels of communication, autonomous navigation, scheduling of tasks and even autonomy of choosing tactics. DARPA has successfully steered and developed many autonomous platforms in the US. The carrier-based autonomous drone, Northrop Grumman X-47B could even carry out a mid-air refuelling. The advent of swarm technology coupled with AI would certainly change the way we fight the war in future. Both manned and unmanned aircraft can jointly undertake missions in sync.

Classification

NATO has classified the military drones as Class I, II and III with respect to the size and endurance. Anything weighs below 150 Kg is class I and the drones weighing between 150 kg to 600 Kg are underclass II. These drones are tactical in nature. The strategic ones are the ones weighing beyond 600 Kg, which come under the class III. The roles of the drone in the military were confined to reconnaissance, combat mission includes weapon delivery and as decoy targets. Majority of the military UAV platforms are under the class II and III.

Of late DARPA has started focussing on Fast Lightweight Autonomy (FLA) program, which is a clear indication of the growing relevance of small drones. The possibilities of class I drones in military applications are being explored in this article. Academia and incubators can focus on developing these applications in the years to come to support our Armed Forces.

Suicide Drones

Suicide drones are going to trigger a Revolution in Military Affairs (RMA) in the coming years. Stealthy suicidal drones can fly low by carrying a payload of detonators and fly to the designated target with a high level of precision. This can even enter a closed area under a roof or a bunker and detonate. Such drones can be tailored and customised suiting to the battlefield and missions being carried out.

Drones for Night Vision

Micro or small drones weighing a few grams can be a buddy to a soldier which can be launched during dark hours to map the terrain ahead prior advancement of troops. These drones with Forward Looking Infrared Cameras (FLIR) cameras can give live clear pictures of the terrain ahead for safe night missions.

Drones for Laser Target Designation

Small VTOL (Vertical Take-Off and Landing) drones can also be mounted with a laser gun payload that can detect and designate the target in pitch dark conditions. The laser coupled weapon delivery system can guide the rocket/ missile to the designated target.

Low Altitude Synthetic Aperture Radar (SAR) Drones

SAR radars are used for large-area high-resolution images in cloudy and pitch-dark conditions. All military satellites and high-flying military reconnaissance UAVs are fitted with these radars. These radars use the principle of artificially enhancing the radar antenna aperture for obtaining high-resolution images. In order to map the movements of enemy installations/vehicles/troops across the border, low altitude drones with SAR capabilities coupled with AI can be used in the dark hours.

Bionic Birds

Birds flying across the border can be lethal in the coming years. It is very difficult to catch bionic birds on radar or camera. In areas where bird activities are more, identifying bionic birds among other birds are nearly impossible.

As Chaff and Flares

A whole range of deception and decoy systems can be articulated and designed by drones for countermeasure operations. It can even carry pyros for flares and misguide enemy radars and incoming missiles by launching chaffs. Sacrificing a drone in lieu of an expensive military platform would always be a better option for a fighting force. This system can be deployed at sea also.

Over The Horizon (OTH) Communication Transceiver

Line of sight is always a constraint in V/UHF military communication systems due to uneven terrains. Erecting a mobile communication tower needs mobilisations and cannot be done in a stealthy manner on hilly terrain. VTOL drones with OTH transceivers could do the trick for military troops. On an as-required basis, the troops can launch the drone to a predetermined altitude. The drone can be made airborne for a set duration of time to facilitate the communication successfully.

OTH Navaid for Advancing Troops

Hostile uneven terrain is always a challenge for troops to navigate and progress their missions. VTOL drones with adequate sensors can move ahead and always act as a guide to the troops on the move.

Land Mine Detection

Drones fitted with Ground Penetrating Radar (GPR) using software-defined radio (SDR) platform can be a game-changer in exploring the already planted landmines. Since detecting and defusing mines is a hazardous exercise, drones are the best bet for these hostile missions.

Transporting Weapon Logistics/Spares and Medical Support

It is also wiser to use drones for supporting troops deployed in the forward areas of uneven terrain. Introducing VTOL drones to lift different payloads could be explored in the days to come. If Amazon can do drone delivery in cluttered cities, why not we design ruggedised drones for military transportation. We can create fleets of drones as a support system for providing logistic supply for frontline troops deployed on mountain tops and hostile terrains.

Swarm Attack

A swarm of cheap detonating drones launched across the border could be always a disaster for the enemy. It is very difficult to detect and destroy these disposable drones. This model of the offensive is stealthy, lethal and cheap to execute.

SAR at Sea

Search and Rescue (SAR) at sea is always a challenge for the Indian Navy. A delay in a SAR mission could be detrimental in saving the life of drowning casualties. Shipborne VTOL drones would certainly help in tracking the floating debris beyond visual range from the rescue ship.

Drones Mounted with Automated Guns

Gun mounted drones can be used as an airborne platform to infiltrate and destroy enemy positions. These drones can be designed with appropriate recoil stabilisation. Aerial drones are any time better than the land robots for missions including counter-insurgency operations. Swarming these drones to take up frontline attack would be an RMA in the years to come.

Drones for Anti-Submarine Warfare (ASW)

The submarines are stealthy and very lethal at sea. They always pose a serious threat to naval vessels at sea. Tracking enemy submarines is a big challenge using sonobuoys and depth charges. But when we need to cover a large area in ASW operations, ship-borne drones swarms could become handy in establishing communications between floating sonobuoys to the mother ships or even ASW aircraft under operations.

High Resolution Aerial Optical Camera

Nano drones can also be exploited for daylight operations by mounting high-resolution aerial cameras. This also can be designed as a pocket-sized buddy for the soldiers set on a mission.

Conclusion

The initiative by DGCA by bringing in the 'Digital Sky' and 'NPNT' (No permission No Take off) regulations can help only safe flying of drones in the civil airspace. These initiatives are mere regulations and are not going to directly help the drone industry to take-off. India lags in drone technologies associated with the military. Time has come for the drone manufacturers and enthusiasts to look into the varied applications available in the military domain and support Indian Armed Forces.

14. Mitigating Drone Threats

Lt Col Nikhil Srivastava

The Unmanned Aerial System consists of three components, a remote-controlled aircraft, a ground-based controller, and a communication link with the UAV. The drones are controlled remotely by a human operator with various degrees of autonomy. Fully autonomous UAVs have no provision for human intervention and enjoy the highest level of autonomy.

Drones can also be used as attack craft for suicidal missions. Before we move on to the topic at hand a brief classification as to the type of drones needs to be known. These are described in the succeeding paragraph.

Various Classifications

The Drones can be classified with respect to Weight, Endurance, and Levels of Autonomy. They are as under:-

Weight

Class 1 - Under 150 kgs

Class 2 - Between 150 to 600 kgs

Class 3 - Above 600 kgs

Endurance and Altitude of Operation

Tier 1 - Low Altitude Long Endurance (LALE)

Tier 2 - Medium Altitude Long Endurance

Tier 3 - High Altitude Long Endurance

Levels of Autonomy

There are six levels of Autonomy

Level 0 - Basic Assistance; Drone is controlled manually with assistance from the drone for safe flight

Level 1 - Low-level automation and advanced assistance; The drone is able to automate landing and/ or return to home base in an open area

Level 2 - Partial Automation; The drone can reliably execute planned grid flights with little to no pilot inputs

Level 3 - Conditional autonomy. Specific mission types are automated by the drone. The pilot remains as an emergency override

Level 4 - Partial Autonomy. The pilot provides mission intent and parameters, then remains aware as a fallback system during flight

Level 5 - Full autonomy with AI-based reinforcement learning. The pilot may start the mission remotely, optionally with an abort button

Threat from Drones

Drones today can be a toy for hobbyists, a tool for commerce and logistics and a multi-purpose, multi-dimensional platform for security and military applications. Drone ranges from miniature ones carrying small payloads to huge drones that can launch Hellfire missiles.

But drone technology has a dark side too. They can be used for Industrial espionage by interdicting into rival companies wifi and cable connections. The threat from suicidal drones across the border could be disastrous for frontline forces. In the hands of terrorists, they could become a very potent weapon. It can be used as suicidal drones to attack public gatherings, sports events, religious festivals, and any scenario one can think of. It can also be used to target individuals in a crowd. The assassination of the Iranian General Qasem Soleimani is a classical example.

There are three threat categories of these drones. The first threat is in the form of a drone attack; drones carrying explosives, dirty bombs can hit vital Installations including Nuclear sites, critical facilities, populated areas, or events with large gatherings. The second threat is that of eavesdropping, espionage and tracking using high powerful cameras and other devices which can eavesdrop into conversations and transmissions through wifi or even cable networks. The third threat is the one being employed by our western adversary, using drones to smuggle in contraband, weapons, drugs, and even counterfeit money.

Countering the Drone Threat

Challenges

The expanding drone technology and its increasing autonomy poses serious challenges in mitigating the threat posed by this system. The UAVs' ability to travel through the air could overcome most of the 'traditional' physical barriers. UAVs poses a very wide range of threats of which each one would require a unique mitigation approach.

The regulatory challenges impose special licensing for those in possession of drones and for the pilots to fly these machines. Depending on their weights, sizes, and employability, there are designated no-fly zones for drones.

Mitigating the Threat

Drones could be a treat if they are in the hands of rogue elements. No number of regulations will stop such elements from wrongdoing. Hence the regulations will have to be given teeth or we should go for the destruction of the drones or even capture these drones. The extirpation of the drone threat will require a deployment of a system across areas where such threats are perceived

Detection and Identification

Detection and Identification are the first step in the process of neutralising drone threats. The structure, acoustics, and size of drones make it very difficult to detect aerial vehicles. According to a North Atlantic Treaty Organization Industrial Advisory Group Study (NATO,2013): "no one sensor type alone is able to provide sufficient tracking and identification capability to offer a reliable and effective defence against the drone threat." The ever-increasing capabilities of drone technologies ensure the usage of several types of detection systems, namely; the reflectance of ultraviolet, visible, and infrared photons; radar reflectance; acoustic emissions; electromagnetic emissions; and induced magnetic fields.

Radars

The radars are mainly used for the detection of aerial objects like Missiles and aircraft, but the classic radar technologies are not suitable for drone detection as they are designed to avoid small objects. However, some Radar technologies can be adapted for drone detection; for example, the Electronic Scanning Radar or the Active Electronically Scanned Array (AESA) radars can be adapted for drone detection. It is a type of phased array radar in which the transmitter and receiver are made of a number of small solid-state modules. The beams are emitted by each element and reflections received by the antenna are reconstructed. Essentially AESA can scan large areas simultaneously without any moving parts (or minimum movement) (Cohen, 1994) (Pike, 2011). AESA—and similar advances in radar detection of small cross-sectional items—has the advantage of being extremely versatile, both in terms of host platforms and detection capabilities. However, with the variation in UAV radar cross-section, even the recent advances in AESA-type detection capabilities will be challenged regularly in detecting UAVs.

Electro-optical Systems

The electro-optical systems are also a potent technology in detecting drones. They have the capability of detecting, tracking, and also identifying a drone through visual contact with the drone. The infrared capabilities of some of these systems can easily distinguish the heat signature between the birds and the drones. Passive visible imaging (e.g., UV, visible and near-infrared) and passive thermal imaging (short-wave, medium wavelength, and long-wavelength infrared) are other electro-optical technologies that can be used in drone detection. The advantages of passive visible imaging include the possibility to distinguish between a UAV, birds, or any other object in the sky fairly inexpensively due to commercial availability. The advantages of the passive thermal imaging devices are the reduction of background signal noise, enhanced nighttime detection, and less susceptibility to weather degradations. However, the disadvantages are the requirement of a clear line of sight, the high susceptibility to the background noise of the passive visible ranging devices, and the low thermal signature of the drones in the case of thermal imaging devices.

Radio Emission

Many of the Drones and sensors use a radio connection to receive commands from a UAV operator through radio communication or transmit data (video feed for example) back to the operator or base station. These emissions can be detected and tracked. The primary advantage of this technology is its independence from light and weather conditions, meaning that detection can be done even in dark conditions or in foggy (rainy) weather. This technology also has the capability to take over the drone by radio spoofing. The disadvantages include the fact that not all UAVs will be emitting radio signals and that some can be set on an autonomous, powerless glide path. Most of the Anti-drone systems in the Market use this technology to detect and interfere with the drones using radio transmissions for control.

Acoustic

Acoustic sensors detect specific noise signatures created by UAV motors and propellers. Despite the advantages of being a passive sensor that is relatively inexpensive, acoustic sensors would make ineffective standalone detection systems (Busset, et al, 2015). For example, these sensors have a limited range, rely on matching registered acoustic sensors to a database of known UAV signatures, suffer from high nuisance alarm rates (especially in urban environments), and are not capable of detecting gliding UAVs as those do not produce any significant noise.

Magnetic Detection Systems

These are systems based on the detection of large metal objects by their influence on electromagnetic fields. These systems are potentially useful only against large UAVs made of metals or having significantly large metal parts, as they are only capable of detecting substantially large metal parts. This system is largely ineffective as most UAVs including smaller drones are now increasingly using carbon fibre frames.

Visual

This is the most effective method of detection as it provides unparalleled classification performance and almost immediate response initiation. However, there is a limit to human endurance and monotony does set in lowering the capabilities substantially over a period of time. Second, the limited nature of visual capability of Humans including vision-enhancing devices.

Neutralization and Destruction

This is the second stage of the mitigation process against drones. This stage involves the neutralization of drones either by capturing or destroying the drones. This involves the response which needs to be given to the attacking or intruding drones; whether to divert, capture or destroy. The choice of the response will be based on the threat perception of the intruding drones and the response capability of the defender. The factors which need to be taken into account would be; first, the interception range should be greater than the stand-off range of the drone to mitigate the damage which can be caused if an explosive carrying drone is destroyed in the air. Second, the detection and the response mechanisms must complement each other.

Capturing

One of the options is to capture the drones without destroying them. This gives the advantage of being able to gather intelligence about the drone, its intention, and its source of origin. If it is a payload-carrying drone you also get hold of the contraband. The methods which can be used for capturing the drones are enumerated in the succeeding paragraphs.

Interfering And Dominating the Radiowave and Navigation Systems

The drones use the GPS and GNSS for navigation and are mostly piloted through the use of radio waves. These can be interfered with to crash the drone or capture the drone to guide it to the desired location by use of Radio spoofing. The jammers can be used to jam the frequencies and cause the drone to crash. However, the drones which have the autonomous capability may not be destroyed or crashed as they can trace their way back to the home station.

UAV to UAV Capture

Use an anti-drone UAV to capture the intruder with a net. Presently this system is being developed by Fortem a USA-based Company. The advantage is that apart from the failure of the mission the captured drone can be analyzed further to decipher more information about the originator. The challenge is the timely detection and deployment of the anti-drone. In the case of swarms, the single anti-drone will be overwhelmed.

Destruction

The other option is the complete destruction of the intruding drone; especially the armed ones like the Turkish Songar Drones. These need to have a standoff to be destroyed or there may be some or extensive collateral damage. Some of the techniques include; lasers, electromagnetic pulse, firearms, surface-to-air missiles, and armed drones.

Lasers

The lasers operate by releasing a high-powered beam of photons on the intruder drone. This is useful against a swarm of drones. These are however costly to manufacture but are cheap to operate. However, it is difficult to keep the laser beam focussed on the moving drone. It is also adversely affected by weather conditions and can cause damage to the surroundings and any humans in the vicinity.

Electro-Magnetic Pulse (EMP)

A powerful EMP beam can disable the electronic components of the intruder drone and cause it to crash. The flip side is that these beams may cause damage to all the electronic installations within their range. Also, an autonomous drone may still escape from it by coming back to its home station.

Firearms

One of the classic approaches as demonstrated on India's Western Borders is to use conventional firearms against intruder Drones. Some anti-aircraft guns have also been adapted to be used against drones. The advantage of this technique is that security forces are already trained and equipped with conventional firearms. The main disadvantage is that this technique poses a danger to the surrounding areas and requires a large amount of ammunition to be expended.

Armed Drones

Armed drones with Assault rifles under-slung can be used to destroy intruders. The technique needs to be combined with detection. Once detected, the armed drone is launched to chase the intruder and shoot to destroy it. However, the detection has to be at a stand-off distance so that it minimizes collateral damage in its own areas. This technology needs to be fine-tuned further with data for autonomous detection and neutralization.

Conclusion

Drones have definitely brought in a revolution in technology and logistics and are going to be a game-changer in all major aspects of human consumption. Once gone into the hands of rogue elements, it could create havoc. Hence, we need to have anti-drone systems that can mitigate these emerging threats.

The present anti-drone system needs a major upgrade to mitigate the threats. Most of the suicidal drones have low acoustic and heat signatures making them almost invisible to the present-day detection systems like radars etc. The Anti-Drone industry has to do much catching up to match the killer drones being developed today.

15. LAWS - Challenge to Humanity

Cdr (Dr) Jayakrishnan N Nair

Lethal Autonomous Weapons Systems (LAWS) are highly sophisticated autonomous military weapon systems with an array of sensor suites and pre-programmed computer algorithms which can independently search, select, designate, track, engage and eliminate hostile targets. These weapon systems, once activated can destroy targets without further human intervention. Hence LAWS on a broad scale can transform the structure of war by bringing in Artificial Intelligence (AI) into systems governing weapons where humans would remain out of the loop. Currently AI-triggered Revolution in Military Affairs (RMA) is happening in the leading military establishments across the world.

Legality and Ethical Concerns

LAWS, often dubbed as "killer robots" can be ethically challenged view lethality and machines replacing humans in taking critical tactical decisions. Owning responsibility for a misfire is the main hurdle in deployment and commissioning of LAWS. LAWS raise a host of philosophical, psychological and legal issues since it is a killer machine having AI embedded with no human control. In fact, these weapons have the potential to disrupt the present conventional way of fighting war. Human rights activists are up in arms to ban LAWS, as they would violate the International Humanitarian Laws (IHL) under the Geneva Convention and International Human Rights Law (IHRL) under Universal Declaration of Human Rights (UDHR). The unrest among employees of Goggle involved in the prestigious 'Project Maven' of Pentagon shows the growing awareness on LAWS among youngsters. 'Project Maven' is an AI based project sponsored by DAPRA, which studies the imagery of battle prone area that would eventually improve the strike capability of drones in the battle prone area.

Evolution and Classification of LAWS

LAWS are evolved over a period of time along with AI. The autonomous elements have increased gradually to reach a point where humans have no role to take a decision whether to engage a target or not (Fig 15.1). LAWS have been evolved or classified into three different categories as shown below. The one in contention is the fully autonomous one where humans are not in the loop while engaging a weapon.

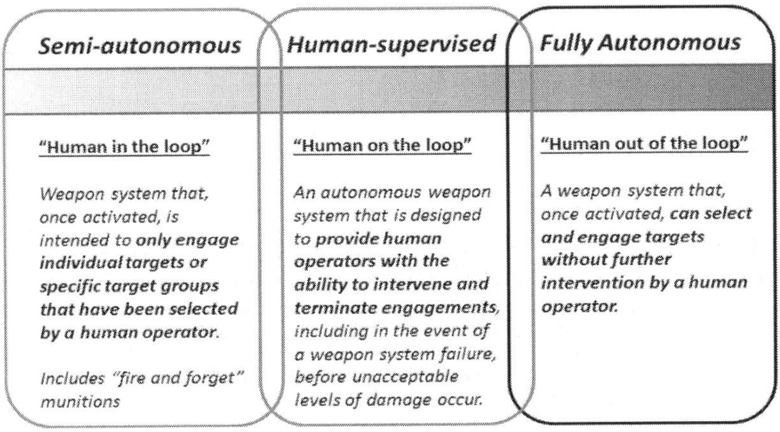

Figure 15.1 PC: https://publications.armywarcollege.edu/pubs/

Current Status of Deployment

Fully-autonomous defensive systems have already been deployed by many advanced countries to intercept enemy air aggression. Defensive weapon systems are deployed to seek all incoming aerial targets. The most common autonomous defensive weaponry is the Missile Defence Systems (MDS). Both US and Israel have deployed and tested MDS successfully. Fire-and-forget systems have been deployed by both UK and Israel. Even South Korea uses the SGR-A1, a sentry robot with an automatic mode, in the Demilitarised border zone with North Korea. Norway's has an offensive autonomous system which will be deployed under the Joint Strike Missile program of NATO. This system can hunt, recognize and detect a target ship or land-based object without human intervention. Both Russia and China are developing similar systems at a faster pace.

Role of AI

AI has become a very competitive emerging technology. AI would become the centre of the global power play triggering a second cold war. The reality today is that AI is leading us towards an algorithmic battleground which has no boundaries or borders and wars will be fought without human involvement. It will be impossible to understand and control this ecosystem in cyberspace and geo-space domain. Machine learning and deep learning would facilitate effective deployment of AI.

New generation GPUs and high-speed hardware with large memory capacity can accelerate the computing speed and perform big data analysis and very high-speed communication.

United Nations and LAWS

Efforts to regulate LAWs have again ended in a stalemate at UN in November 2019. Dialogue happened at UN to address the ramifications of LAWS on human rights. 28 governments demanded a blanket ban on artificial intelligence weapons. But both the US and Russia blocked the move and recommended to form legally binding agreements. During the meeting, member countries of Convention on Conventional Weapons (CCW) could not come in common grounds for a resolution against LAWS. But they have decided to continue the talks for regulating lethal autonomous weapons systems in the next two years. UN diplomats expressed disappointment and blamed Russia for watering down the agenda. Unsatisfied with the lack of progress in the CCW, NGOs have started Campaigning against LAWS, urging countries to bypass the UN convention and to negotiate a separate treaty. In the recently concluded Paris Peace Forum, UN Secretary-General Antonio Guterres again called for a new international treaty to ban LAWs. He stated that "the machines that have the power and discretion to kill without human intervention are politically unacceptable and morally despicable".

Challenges in Cyber Security

The need for a scalable, automated, high-speed vulnerability detection and patching system is growing to make cyber controlled weapons safe. More and more military platforms are getting connected through internet backbone. Embedded software-controlled machines are audited to find the flawed code and vulnerability and correspondingly patches are applied against potential hacking prior deployment. AI/Machine learning (ML) can take up the challenge of automation process of identifying vulnerabilities and simultaneously patching it in the cyber domain. It can simultaneously exploit the vulnerabilities of enemy systems redefining the next level of cyber warfare. There are numerous ways we can increase the autonomy for interaction between conventional and virtual. Cyber operations can be used as a tool to increase the autonomy in conventional weapon systems as well as in countermeasure operations. We can trigger unintended interactions and emergent behaviours between autonomous systems. If not fire-walled adequately, autonomous weapon systems will remain vulnerable to cyber operations.

LAWS – India's Stand

Countries like Russia, China, US, and Israel are spending billions of dollars in the AI research. Artificial intelligence has the potential to transform the combat capabilities of Armed Forces. AI Leadership can always give nations a military edge over adversaries. Amidst calls for a ban on LAWS, India is planning to strengthen their AI-based weapon systems. The recommendation was made by the 17-member newly formed AI task force under Ministry of Defence, which includes members from research organisations, contractors and the military recommends India to enhance AI towards better operational readiness of armed force. The task force has identified few use cases to start with which includes unmanned tanks, under water vessels, aerial vehicles and robotic weaponry. Since India is in nascent stage of development, it is too early to speak about LAWS now.

Conclusion

With the current pace at which the AI being integrated to Military Systems, days are not far where the war machines could become vulnerable and might go out of human control. UN and Human right organisation are sensing this danger and is all out to stop this disaster. Nations will go into a self-destruction mode if they integrate AI into Weapons of Mass Destruction (WMD). LAWS are dangerous systems, once engaged, would trigger counter and counter operations without human interventions. In a nut shell we will live in a world where lethal machines will fight with each other for their respective masters and these masters can seldom control them. There is an imminent requirement to monitor and control the development of LAWS by UN to save the humanity and India has a larger role to play in making LAWS safe.

16. Disruption of Military Warfare

Cdr (Dr) Jayakrishnan N Nair

The connotation **'disruption of military warfare'**, would make many military commanders wonder how the art of fighting war could become a victim of disruptions. The conventional warfare strategies currently adopted by Armed Forces are regimental, foolproof, time tested and would follow some laid down Standard Operating Procedures (SOP) devised out of professional acumen harnessed over the years. Currently, the Armed Force of leading military powers orchestrate their war in a way accustomed to their traditions and experience. The strategies and tactics being adopted by forces during the course of war are evolved out of the training they imbibed from their military academies and war colleges.

Conventional warfare may get disrupted by the advent of new methodologies, distributed command, state of art weapon systems and out of the box tactics. Planning, deployment, resource allocation and surveillance will be taken over by decision support systems powered by Artificial Intelligence. The warfare currently adopted by each nation is unique and differs from one another, view the kind of weapons, type of platforms, the potency of weapons, force level, the structure of command and control, technology etc. Biological weapons and cyber warfare may play a larger role in future wars. The disruption triggered by innovation would bring an element of surprise to adversaries.

The Relevance

Off late the disruptive technology has started playing a larger role in the preparation and conduct of warfare. Indirectly it implies that the conduct of current warfare is likely to go for an overhaul. Speed, precision and lethality would define the course of the war. Battle casualties are likely to come down in future wars. Foot soldiers will be deployed only if there is a pressing requirement. Artificial Intelligence (AI) in military applications and smart weapons would change the entire discourse of warfare. Algorithms will provide the best possible tactic to overcome the adversary with the available resources at the shortest possible time. Advanced 24x7 surveillance systems and decision support systems can speed up the process and cut short the time of engagement.

It is very hard for war pundits to apprehend the fact that their role has been taken over by an AI-powered decision support system. The SOPs, institutional memory and the tactics would have been mapped by AI-based algorithms to assist the command in decision making. Surveillance will play a critical role in future wars. Real-time data collection and analytics will be done round the clock to support the AI systems, which would eventually render superior tactical decisions.

Shortfalls in Conventional Warfare

Conventional warfare has many shortfalls. The error of judgement, wrong perception and poor surveillance can amount to setbacks during war. Poor preservation of institutional memory, the retirement of experienced hands, low shelf life of weapon systems, maintaining a large number of trained soldiers, delay in taking decisions, poor surveillance, delay in the processing of incoming data are few shortfalls of conventional warfare.

Disruptive Technologies

Disruptive technologies are the building blocks of a disruptive force. Artificial Intelligence, Internet of Battlefield Things, robotics, Space Colonization, Virtual Reality, Simulation, Autonomous systems, Cloud-based systems, Hypersonic and Direct Energy Weapons, etc can reboot the current warfare methodology. Innovations in technology and application would become a key element in bringing in surprise to adversaries during the course of the war. Stealth technology and deception will add a new dimension to the war. Advanced sensors, Augmented Reality, Wearable devices, Unmanned Ground Vehicles (UGV) would lift the battlefield tactics to the next level. Cyber-warfare can spread propagandas that could influence war strategists. Space-based systems would replace many defence infrastructures on the ground and at sea.

How to Embrace Disruption

Disruption view AI is a necessary evil for all Armed Forces. We have to align our forces towards embracing new technologies. Front line soldiers will be deployed only for surgical or tailored missions where machines cannot handle the complexities. Training would play a major role in embracing new methodologies. Forces have to re-orient their training curriculum to cater to the new challenges in learning Industry 4.0 and strategic technologies. Human lives are going to be more valuable in days to come. Re-training of existing soldiers essential to the progress adoption of new methods.

Disruption Technologies and Systems

Sr.	Conventional Warfare Systems	Disruption Systems
a	Fighter Jets	Weapon drones/ Precision Missiles
b	Manned surveillance aircraft	High-altitude long-range surveillance drones/ Surveillance satellites
c	Aircraft Interceptor	Missile Shield/ Anti air missiles
d	Land/ Sea-based surveillance radars	Long range surveillance drones/ Surveillance satellites
e	War Ships/Submarines	All electric autonomous ships with specific roles
f	Tanks	Unmanned Ground Vehicles mounted with weapon launcher
g	Active surveillance	24X7 passive surveillance
h	Foot soldiers	Swarm mini drones, bots, Tech soldiers
i	Artillery	High precision missiles and weaponized robotic vehicles
j	War room commanders	Decision support systems
k	Commando Operations	Missile Drones/UGV/mini drones/smart bombs
l	Conventional short-range missiles	Directed Energy Weapons (DEWs) and force fields
m	Hardware based systems based conventional computing	Systems base don quantum computing
n	Personal Protection and communication equipment	Wearables, Internet of Battlefield Things

Conclusion

After the advent of Artificial Intelligence, every embedded system has become a suitable candidate to migrate to an autonomous system. The amalgamation of disruptive technologies would amount to a sea change in battlefield preparation. Autonomous systems could replace manned missions in the future. Tactical decisions rendered by AI-based decision support systems will be more rational, optimal and less emotional. Machines and humans will team up to fight the adversaries in future wars.

17. 6G Technology of China: Impact on Indian Military

Dr Vijay Sakhuja

6G communication technology will place China ahead of many western countries. This technology will have a great impact on India's defence preparedness.

China successfully put into orbit the world's first 6G or Sixth Generation wireless communications technology test satellite in November 2020 to study "6G physics in the environment of space with terahertz electronics". This 70-kilogram satellite named Star Era-12 was launched from the Taiyuan Satellite Launch Center in Shanxi using a Long March-6 rocket. According to South China Morning Post, the satellite will be used to "build smart cities, for disaster prevention and mitigation, and for environmental protection". The 6G technology is expected to be ready by 2030 and could be first put to use for mobile telephony.

Technical Assessment

6G is a major breakthrough in the terahertz space communication segment. The download speed could be as high as one terabyte per second as compared with 600MB for 5G which is four times faster than 4G (LTE). Put simply, a "6G iPhone will download a high-definition movie in 8 seconds and 1,500 high-resolution photos in less than a minute". Furthermore, it could offer "lossless transmission in space to achieve long-distance communications with smaller power output" and close to zero latency.

6G will support intelligent architecture comprising of large-dimension and autonomous networks that integrate space, air, ground, and underwater networks to provide continuous and unlimited wireless connectivity. However, 6G involves the use of new frequency ranges (100 and 500 Gigahertz that must be necessarily tested in space due to high-frequency bands), innovative infrastructure, and enhanced integration of "space-air-ground-sea communication technologies" and scientists fear that 6G could impact "public health, or be too expensive for researchers to use".

In China, the 6G technology is being developed independently by Huawei, ZTE and China Unicorn, and the Chinese government has also set up a research unit that is supported by 37 experts from universities, research institutes and technology companies that will support its development. These specialists are associated with the 6G research blueprint and would offer policy advice. Apparently, China has two teams working on 6G technology since November 2019.

6G technology is still evolving and would need to overcome many technical challenges in basic research, hardware design including its environmental impact (given that 5G attracted adverse environmental and human challenges) before it becomes viable for commercial use.

Geopolitical Considerations

By all counts, China has taken lead in wireless communications technology while the US-led wireless industry is still struggling with 5G. In October 2020, several top companies and global wireless network operators announced the 'Next G Alliance' (NGA) which will focus on R&D, manufacturing, standardization and market readiness of both 5G and 6G (Fig 17.1). The NGA's goal is to "advance North American mobile technology leadership in 6G and beyond over the next decade while building on the long-term evolution of 5G." The NGA could also boast of being entirely free of Chinese influence.

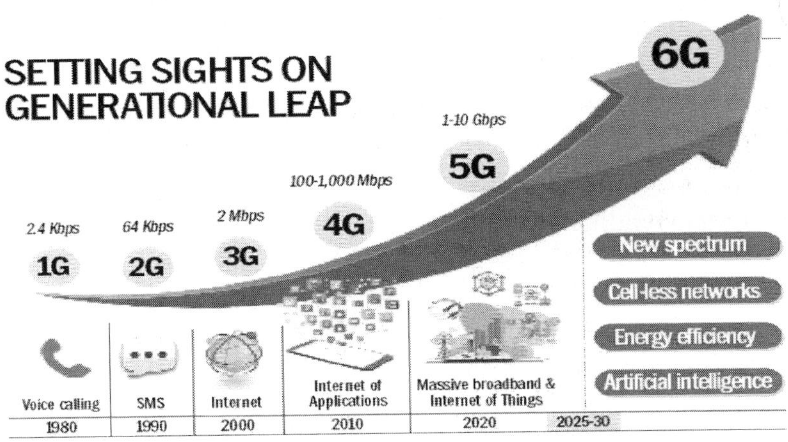

Fig17.1 PC :www.tribuneindia.com/news/comment/mission-6g

6G may be a technological marvel but it is sure to attract geopolitical undercurrent and these could be similar to 5G led by Huawei and ZTE. Both were under scrutiny in many European countries, Australia, India and the US and continue even today. The US even enacted the Foreign Investment Risk Review Modernization Act in August 2018 which notes that a country of "special concern that has a demonstrated or declared strategic goal of acquiring a type of critical technology or critical infrastructure that would affect United States leadership in areas related to national security." It is fair to argue that the 6G competition has all the ingredients of geopolitics and geostrategic contestation flavoured with technological rivalries involving an "an arms-technology race" and will attract an "army of researchers on it to remain competitive".

Military

It has been noted that 6G will have a "major impact on military practices, such as war formation, equipment development, and battlefield communications... Promoting the gradual application of 6G in the military might be one of the major focuses for the Chinese armed forces to adapt to the new military changes in the future." 6G will be a key enabler for any information military. It would help in the development of cutting-edge AI systems that can crunch through vast amounts of data that the military receives through a multitude of sensors and sources for its operations. It will enable real-time analytics, provide commanders solutions or courses of action based on the influx of data the military receives, cut latency, and cull out the most suitable data to enable an effective kinetic response.

A vast network of sensors, robots and autonomous vehicles would be connected through sophisticated artificial intelligence, which could be the future of faster, deadlier, and may be partial autonomous warfare. Reportedly, a robot should be able to "search for a wounded soldier left on the battlefield".

It is a potential conduit for the PLA to leapfrog and gain ascendency over its arch-rival the US military. The US Department of Defense has announced a pan-military AI Strategy which lays out the imperatives for the integration of AI across all arms of the US armed forces. It set up the Joint Artificial Intelligence Center (JAIC) to "preserve and expand military advantage".

PLA and 6G

By 2030 the PLA would potentially be riding high on the 4IR technology (Artificial Intelligence (AI), Machine Learning (ML), Big Data, cloud computing, Augmented Reality, Quantum Computing, Cognitive Computing (CC) and Internet of Things (IoT)) wave and could emerge as a potent 6G-enabled force. It will be highly digitalized-inteligized that would serve both as the 'ordnance' and tool of 'deterrence'.

The 6G would be the core of the PLA's strategic network consisting of a large number of platforms that could be floating in the space-near space, flying in the air, on the surface and deep-diving-autonomous underwater vessels, for conducting large scale surveillance, reconnaissance and exploration. At the tactical level, 6G would facilitate real-time targeting, AI-enabled decisions by the tactical commander, and swift data exchange between the sensors and shooter.

However, PLA would experience challenges of human resources due to the ageing Chinese population (by 2030, China will be an ageing society with the world's highest proportion of people over 65), slowing economic growth (moderate reforms-average annual growth would reach 5.1% in the 2020s, then 2.9% in the 2030s) thus rising costs to maintain the military. These would necessitate diverting spending from the military to the welfare and health care of the people.

This weakness will be offset by a 'lightly manned' yet 'highly lethal force' of unmanned-autonomous platforms. However, PLA will be confronted with "legal and ethical issues" concerning whether to give unbridled control to machines to make decisions to kill, injure, or destroy. China has not announced whether it is pursuing lethal autonomous weapon systems (LAWS), but it has certainly argued that LAWS merit the attention of the international community.

Implication for Indian Military

The PLA's march towards a 4IR-enabled force would require an imaginative yet powerful Indian matrix of the military-industrial complex that can produce/ support 4IR enabled military platforms, an innovative military strategy and a highly skilled human resource. These will be critical for delivering a battle-winning advantage.

At the policy level, a modest beginning has been made after the government set up a 17-member multi-stakeholder task force for Strategic Implementation of Artificial Intelligence for National Security and Defence (2018) with a mandate to explore the use of AI in offensive and defensive operations concerning aviation, naval, land systems, cyber, nuclear and biological warfare arenas.

The Indian defence establishment has taken note of the ongoing proliferation of 4IR technologies among many militaries of the world. However, they will have to reassess the future requirements of conventional assets. The remedy lies in both rethinking priorities as also the design of future hardware-software focused on 4IR.

A good start point would be to study in details the Syrian battleground and more recently the Azerbaijani–Armenian clashes which exposed the vulnerability of traditional (armoured, mechanized, and motorized) formations pitted against drone warfare weaponry. 'Drone – artillery complexes' on land and 'transitioning from manned fleet infrastructure to a mix of both manned and unmanned platforms' would be useful choices. It is not surprising that most of the advanced militaries are planning a mix of manned and unmanned forces with a visible tilt towards unmanned platforms which would necessarily have 6G architecture at its core for battle efficiency and efficient operational and logistics management.

India's strategic partnership with the US and Japan envisages cooperation in emerging technologies and 6G technology merits joint development. In their summit meeting earlier this year, the Quad Member States agreed to "partner to address the challenges presented by new technologies and collaborate to set the norms and standards that govern the innovations of the future". In this context, it would be prudent that India's national and other private telecom players explore joining the NGA and fill the gap resulting from the late introduction of 5G in India.

Finally, whoever controls the network, controls the world. In the 19th century, Britain was the leader of the commercial telegraph, then in the 21st century, China is the 5G King and could continue its leadership with regard to 6G while the NGA develops its own 6G.

18. Development of Fully Autonomous Military Systems

Cdr (Dr) Jayakrishnan N Nair

After the advent of Artificial Intelligence (AI), few advanced nations are busy in developing and deploying an array of autonomous weapon systems to attain better speed and accuracy. All fatal missions are likely to be undertaken by unmanned systems in future. AI based Tactical Decision Support Systems (TDSS) could replace a commander in the war rooms. AI triggered smart weapons will replace the conventional warheads.

Fully autonomous weapon systems are the ones which can process and exploit available data to arrive at decisions with the help of pre-programmed algorithms to make choices and act logically in unanticipated circumstances independently, more importantly, within the ethical framework rendering minimum collateral damage. The design and development of fully autonomous systems is a challenge to the leading military powers view underlying complexity in making it fail safe. Fully autonomous systems imply zero human intervention once let off. Advances in computational techniques and sensor technology accelerated the development of fully autonomous systems.

Accountability of collateral damage inflicted by fully autonomous weapon systems is a matter of contention. Machines can be made as scapegoats for all failed missions. Fully autonomous weapon systems are very effective in Narrow AI circumstances where the application is calibrated. Currently risk aversion has become a big barrier for enhancing the degree of autonomy of weapon systems.

Fully Autonomous vs Supervised Autonomous vs Semi-Autonomous Systems

Fully autonomous weapon systems are the ones when activated, can select and engage targets without any further intervention by the humans. They are less supervised autonomous weapon systems where the human operators cannot override operation of the weapon system. The system can select and engage targets without any human intervention after activation. Whereas supervised autonomous weapon systems are the ones designed to intervene by human operators and even to terminate the engagement in case of system failure. Semi-autonomous weapon systems are the one intended for specific target group. It has the provision to override the weapon delivery system post-delivery by humans.

Advantages of Fully Autonomous Weapon Systems

Only human beings show the indiscipline by deliberately deviating from the set rules and regulations which they are supposed to follow. Fully autonomous weapon systems are less emotional than human beings during combat or in a hostile environment. A robotic machine cannot hate or fear or be emotional or become tired. It has no survival instinct. The robot can delay the use of force for the most appropriate moment to destroy the target. They can sense and process more information simultaneously faster than human brains and hence it is wiser for humans to delegate many tasks to machines to avoid multitasking and information overload during wartime.

Fully autonomous systems are most appropriate for Narrow Artificial Intelligence AI. Their requirements are more desirable for distinguishing between military and non-military assets and determining the legitimacy of targets. They are fool proof in comparison and can take better proportionality decisions than humans. They are adaptable to changing circumstances and are capable to face unanticipated circumstances from enemy side. These systems are controlled by preset algorithms catering all eventualities.When evera new situation arises, the system would switch over to the learning mode and the new learning would be used for future engagements.

Choice of Autonomous System

Majority of the AI based autonomous systems are currently semi-autonomous in nature. If these systems are rendering results to the satisfaction, there is no need to upgrade them to fully autonomous systems.There are certain applications where both manned systems and unmanned systems can team up as peers. The decision to migrate from semi-autonomous to fully autonomous system should be taken after detailed deliberation since the right to abort a mission is impossible.

Identifying Use Cases

Identifying use cases for fully autonomous system needs detailed deliberations and input from various domain experts. Fully autonomous systems found to be ideal for defending airspace, land borders and coastal lines. But developing these systems exclusively for penetrating enemy defence needs extensive research and studies. Meeting military objectives by giving immunity to civilian population is most important factor being considered while short listing use cases for fully autonomous military systems.

Challenges in Design and Development

a. Irreversible System

The very fact that we cannot recall a fully autonomous system post launch makes it more challenging for the weapon developers. Since these weapons are irreversible, the reach of fully autonomous systems should be calibrated within the frame work of safety of mankind and magnitude of human causality. Owning up responsibility for malfunction, accidents and collateral damages by the nation who launched the weapon is a big challenge.Precautions are mandatory to avoid civilian causalities

b. Limitations of Algorithms

The algorithms used for high resolution image analysis, information storage and decision making are very complex and resource intensive. The system should have adequate redundant channels to boost the reliability of system. The quantum of algorithms needs to be executed consecutively is limited by the computational capability and system memory.

c. Limitations of Sensors

The accuracy of algorithms being executed is depended on the quality of weapon sensors. Weapon sensors includes Optical Camera, LASER, GPS, Infrared and Light Detection and Ranging (LIDAR). The size of sensors limits the capability of autonomous systems. Adding better sensor could make the system bulkier and hence optimization of size and volume could become a trade-off. Moreover, high resolution sensors warrant large memory capacity and better computational powers.

d. Hardware Limitations

High resolution terrain mapping of autonomous systems is resource intensive. Same is applicable for the underwater sonic mapping as well as for airspace surveillance and mapping. Processing of images is throttled by the capacity of system memory and speed of Graphic Processor Unit (GPU). Hardware capability limits the speed of autonomous system and the level of automation. Only few manufacturers exist in the world who can produce the 'mil std' hardware with high processing capacity.

e. Band width of Data Link

Limitations of band width of wireless communication network is another choking point for data link between weapons and controlling platforms. Band width capacity limits the speed of system and the level of automation. Military uses 30 to 88 MHz band for close air support and associated data links. Limitations in communication hardware limits the band width to a large extend.

f. Availability of Domain Experts

Technologies associated with fully autonomous systems are robotics, optics, artificial intelligence, machine learning, deep learning, validation, quality assurance, sensors calibration, cyber security and material science. Availability of domain experts in each field under one roof is a big challenge for weapon manufacturers.

g. Harsh Battlefield Environment

The process of terrain mapping of land, under water and airspace is an exhaustive resource intensive exercise. Unpredictability of terrains and moving weapon platforms of enemy, adds to the complexity of algorithms for fully autonomous platforms. Making them weather proof and adding more redundant channels are mandatory to avoid mission failures. Autonomous platforms are designed to overcome unprecedented obstructions in transit during missions.

h. Interference from Other Systems

Cross Interference of sensor signals is another big challenge for fully autonomous systems. Currently lasers and radars are used for navigation of autonomous platforms. Spurious Signals from external systems can always play spoilsport and implications could be disastrous. There can be deliberate attempts by the enemy in some form of Electronic Counter Measures (ECM) to misguide the autonomous systems.

i. Time Constraints

Time plays a major role in autonomous system efficiency. Algorithms are capable of successful planning and re-planning of mission activities within the time frame. Interpretation of onboard and offboard sensor information should happen in time for speedy decision-making process. Effective command-and-control squarely depends on timely processing of mission data and sharing them to stake holders.

j. Testing Stage

Testing is one of the most difficult stage in fully autonomous weapon system development. The process is time consuming and the designers may have to go back to the design board many times. Wrong choice of use cases and the flaws of design can have serious ramifications in testing stage. The testing and trial process is humongous since there is a need to mobilize massive military resources.

Conclusion

Protest by few nations against autonomous weapon systems at UN is a big challenge for fully autonomous weapon developers since the stakes are high. The fear of miscarriage is the biggest barrier in the development of fully autonomous systems. Nevertheless, days are not far where we humans will team up with machines as peers for military operations.

19. Algorithmic Warfare

Cdr (Dr) Jayakrishnan N Nair

Algorithmic warfare is a warfare which is driven by autonomous systems powered with Artificial Intelligence (AI) that can control the weapon platforms, systems, operations and even tactics in a network centric battlefield. Algorithms are sequence of instructions and rules that computer machines use to solve problems. Algorithms can be as simple as a decision tree or a complex set of instructions governing the autonomy of weapon systems.

Human lives are becoming more valuable over the years. Induction of unmanned autonomous systems into the battle field could eventually improve the speed and accuracy of weapon systems as well as bring down the battle field causalities. Major military powers are currently planning to switch to algorithmic warfare making combat actions faster than the decision-making speed of humans. A better algorithm will ensure technical superiority over adversaries in processing, analysing and rendering solutions.

In an Algorithmic Warfare, the solutions provided by algorithms would shape the military judgements, tactics and decisions. In short, the 'Intelligent Machines' or 'Killer Robots' will fight the war for their respective masters. We are now entering into a new era of RMA (Revolution of Military Affairs) and MTR (Military Technical Revolution).

Artificial Intelligence and Algorithmic Warfare

Artificial Intelligence (AI) is a man-made intelligent system with skills such as learning, reasoning and solving problems. In Algorithmic Warfare, both weapon platforms and military assets fielded by the fighting force would form a part of the AI based battlefield network. The specific task of weapon systems and associated platforms engaged in war would be designated by complex algorithms in the time and space domain.

There is always an element of surprise for enemy by virtue of the speed and accuracy at which smart weapons are operated. Intelligent machines are capable of self-learning and rendering optimised output suiting to the tactical situation.

Machine learning (ML) is inherent in AI and the system with integrated neural network would learn continuously and evolve during operations.

Ethical Issue

There are many ethical, moral and legal issues associated with algorithmic warfare which is driven by AI and Machine Intelligence (MI). Most of the autonomous weapons fall under the ambit of 'Lethal Autonomous Weapon Systems' (LAWS). Many nations have rallied against LAWS at the United Nation. Efforts are on by human right activist groups at UN to institute a complete ban on development of autonomous weapon systems. Nevertheless, leading military powers continue their research and development on AI based weapon systems.

Cost Factor

Military operations are lethal and can lead to loss of human lives. Availability of combat manpower for military operations would decline in the coming years. Since the cost of man power is increasing year after year, advanced nations are planning to do away with the expensive conventional war preparation and switch to Algorithmic Warfare. The cost of maintenance of defence personnel is going up every year. Unmanned autonomous systems could be a great option available for nations to reduce the overheads and minimise battle field causalities.

Autonomy to Sub-systems

During a combat, military command would engage with many weapons and sensor systems simultaneously. It is humanly impossible for the command to control and monitor supplementary systems along with core weapon/tactical system. Hence forth by rendering autonomy to sub-systems would help the command/crew to focus on the core operation leaving the peripheral systems under the control AI.

Disruption in Conventional War Fighting

AI powered autonomous systems can change the conventional way of fighting war and may change some established precepts in future. The new approach would even force the military command to re-structure the fighting force. The size of an armed force may become irrelevant compared to the battle being fought. Wealthy small states could field more potent forces than the large populous nations. Intelligent machines may reorient the forces and minimise the advantages of some states with respect to their experience and skill. Majority of the unmanned autonomous weapon systems deployed can be expendable. More miniaturised stealthy weapon platforms will come into fray in future.

Use Cases

Currently there are many AI based autonomous systems in the field of navigation, tactics, self-protection, weapon guidance and communications. AI is being introduced into many areas including cyber-security, logistics/ transportation, target recognition, health care, simulation, training, threat monitoring, tactical situation analysis, prediction and data analytics.

Engaging enemy drones and aircraft, integration of tank guns with sensors, coordinating resupply and maintenance of military assets, planning and installation artillery barrages, fusion of different sensor feeds together into a coherent picture and analysing/Identifying identifying blind spots in enemy defence are few applications where in AI has delivered positive results.

We can broadly classify autonomous systems into two categories. Autonomy achieved at rest and the autonomy while in motion. The one at rest is superior and virtual which would facilitate and control the entire battle order at a higher level. The one in motion refers to the autonomy of moving platforms and weapons. Both categories combine to form a coherent autonomous entity while engaging in a war.

Network Centric Algorithmic Warfare

Network centric warfare has improved the coordination between fighting units and speeded up the data exchange between platforms and command. Protocols were laid for seamless communication between heterogeneous systems and interoperability of divergent platforms for utmost precision and speed. Networks are excellent in collecting, storing and sharing information but less useful in processing and delivering useful insights to command.

Networking of autonomous platforms is the next level of integration; wherein multi-dimensional divergent platforms synergies to form a combined force in a battle field. Visual data capture and analysis are key for decision making and successful missions. Dedicated secured military cloud and standalone captive battle field network mandatory for cyber secure network centric operations.

Integration of Machines and Humans

Both humans and machines have strengths and shortcomings. The notion that machines could replace humans is future is not completely true. In algorithmic warfare, the real implementation involves deployment of an optimum mix of human and machine intelligence together. Battle networks comprise interlinked computer systems programmed for data analytics, information gathering, sensing hostile situations and rendering command which overlays the theatre. AI based systems will be supplemented with Deep Learning neural networks.

AI enabled network thus facilitate weapon systems complemented by a large number of low-cost autonomous unmanned systems designed for specific tasks. The unmanned systems are designed and fielded for unique tasks and are expendable, hence could be risked for dangerous missions in lieu of manned platforms.

Challenges

The main challenge in deploying AI based systems is the lack of reliable data for drawing meaningful conclusion. Collection of useful data for analytics may take many years. Integration, testing and deploying of autonomous weapons safely is a big challenge. Initial cost involved in development of systems and generating meaningful solutions will be very high. Only few manufactures in the world can provide military standard hardware support to meet the requirements. Identifying suitable development teams for AI platforms is another challenge which cannot be undermined.

AI based systems are not flexible and are incapable of handling minor changes in context. AI systems have poor domain adaptability and hence they struggle to apply knowledge learned in one context to another. Humans generally make better judgements in situations of high complexity and uncertainty. This means that amalgamating men and machine would be optimal and can become more potent.

Conclusion

Advancement of AI is irreversible and Algorithmic Warfare will become a disruption to the existing conventional warfares. Application of Artificial Intelligence and Machine Intelligence has increased manifold in the recent years for a wide range of military applications. Algorithmic Warfare could trigger seamless integration of military assets and associated tasks. This warfare can also impact the design and development of weapon platforms in future. Russian President Vladimir Putin recently declared that 'whoever becomes the leader in the AI sphere, will become the ruler of the world'.

20. Electromagnetic Propulsion for Military and Space Applications

Dr KRM Nair

Electromagnetic Propulsion (EMP) technology's potential for military applications are currently being explored by many nations. Magnetic-driven precision staging devices, large mass catapult launchers, low-speed and high-speed trains and cargo movers, high-speed long-range fire support naval guns, high-speed satellite launches, and EMP-propelled ships and submarines are few of the applications that are currently being tried out. The discovery of the concept of Electromagnetic Propulsion was in 1889 by Prof. Elihu Thomson. In the 1960s E.R.Laitwaite developed the linear induction motor which used the application of the EMP.

Concept

Electromagnetic Propulsion (EMP) consists essentially of two components, one is the electromagnet where electricity is used to generate a magnetic field and the second is propulsion, the process of propelling (pushing) something. EMP, therefore, is the principle of accelerating an object by using the flow of magnetic field and current. When current flows through a conductor in a magnetic field, the conductor experiences a force in a direction perpendicular to the current and the magnetic field known as Lorenz Force. If a fluid such as a gas or liquid is used instead of the conductor for the propulsion, it is called Magneto Hydro Dynamic drive.

Magnetic Levitation (Maglev)

The principle of a linear motor and the property of magnetic repulsion is used in Maglev trains. The first patent on magnetic levitation transportation system was granted to James Powel and Gordon Danby in 1966, which proposed superconducting Maglev transportation. The first maglev system in the world worked between Birmingham International airport and Birmingham Railway station in the 1990s.

Propulsion of a maglev train (Fig 20.1) is caused by a linear motor, which has all 3 elements of a conventional Direct Current (D.C) motor, i.e., stator, rotor and commutator. If the conventional D.C motor is opened and flattened out, it becomes a linear conceptually. In a maglev system, the track becomes the poles alternating between north and south poles along the length of the track, a solenoid that is propelled along the track (the train) and a commutator to change the poles sequentially. The solenoid can be replaced by permanent magnets.

Fig 20.1 PC:sputnik news

There are three types of magnetic propulsion used for maglev as explained below.

a. Propulsion by Linear Induction Motor

In propulsion by linear induction motor (LIM), the armature becomes the primary winding and the field the secondary winding. The primary (armature) is externally excited and its magnetic field induces currents in the field windings. The primary windings are distributed such that when excited by a 3-phase supply, a travelling field is generated which has forward, backward and pulsating components. The secondary is either a metallic cage or short-circuited 3 phase winding. The current, the primary magnetic field induces into the secondary generates a reactive magnetic field. The interaction of the two fields produces a motion that can be controlled by regulating the phase of the primary current. The armature current can be regulated to control the thrust speed or position. Bearings are used to restrict the motion into a longitudinal single degree of freedom. The LIM where the stator coils are on board is called 'Short Primary" type and where the stator coils are on the guide way and the conducting sheets are on board is called 'Long Primary" type. LIM is used for urban transportation in Japan and similar systems are in use in Malaysia, Canada, New York airport access system etc. LIM requires complex drives to get levitation and causes oscillation.

b. Linear Synchronous Motor Propulsion

The motion of a linear synchronous motor (LSM) is in synchronism with the travelling field produced by a poly-phase armature that is excited by either AC or switched current. The field can be a permanent magnet or variable reluctance system. The propulsion and levitation modules are located on each side of the train. Each module contains the exciting field magnets of the LSM which works as the levitation magnets as well. This system is good for high-speed applications.

c. Propulsion by Permanent Magnets

Permanent magnets have been successfully applied to linear synchronous drives for short distances and for transportation systems in factories etc.. In this system, permanent magnets create the field. The thrust force is generated when the field of the magnets tend to align itself with the travelling field of the armature.

Electromagnetic Rail-guns (EMRG)

Conventional guns use explosives to get the expansion of the gas for launching the projectile. It has limitations of launch velocity and range. Another problem is the safety issue of storing large quantities of explosives. EMRG has advantages over the conventional gun such as enhanced safety as there is no explosive, faster hitting of targets, increased range etc and is a good choice for the Navy.

A rail-gun consists of two parallel metal rails connected to an electric power supply. When a conductive projectile is inserted between the rails the magnetic circuit is completed through it.(Fig 20.2)

The rails become electromagnets and a flux density of the order of 10 Tesla is developed. The current in the rails is in opposite direction. The net magnetic field acts at the right angle to the plane of the rails and produces a Lorenz Force to accelerate the projectile. The force also tries to pull apart the rails and therefore the rails need rigid mounting. EMRG is capable of launching projectiles weighing several kilograms at speeds of Mach 7.

The electrical energy to the rail-gun is given from charged capacitor banks kept near the gun. The charging of the capacitor bank is from a dedicated power supply from the ship's generator system. For launching heavy projectiles over a long distance, the electric power requirement is high. For example, a capacitor bank capable of 10 megajoules capacity can fire 1kg projectile at a speed of 3000 m/sec.

Some of the problems of rail-guns are: -

- The capacitors occupy large space and require maintenance.
- Dedicated power source is required for charging the capacitor bank.
- The rails may get overheated by the high current and the friction from the projectile.

- The electromagnetic field emission from the operation of the gun can be detected by the enemy and require efficient shielding to prevent it.

Fig 20.2 PC: warfare sims

Electric Propulsion Systems for Space applications

The use of electric power enhances the propulsive performance of thrusters used for various space and military applications. Electric Propulsion requires very little mass when compared to the chemical system to accelerate a mass. Some of the technologies are given in this section.

a. Gridded Ion Thruster

In this system, ions are accelerated by electrostatic forces. The electrodes placed at the downstream end of the thruster generate the electric field required for the acceleration. All electrodes have a number of coaxial apertures which act as lenses that electrically focus ions. The upstream electrode is the accelerator grid and is positively charged and the downstream electrode is negatively charged. The ions are attracted towards the accelerator grids creating thousands of ion jets. The exhaust velocity of the ions in the beam is based on the voltage applied.

b. Hall Effect Thruster

Hall Effect Thruster uses the electrostatic potential to accelerate ions to high speeds. The negative charge is provided by the plasma at the open end of the thruster. A radial magnetic field of about 0.03 Tesla is used to confine the electrons. A propellant such as xenon gas is fed through the anode which is diffused into the channel of the thruster where it is ionized by the high energy electrons. The xenon ions are accelerated between the anode and cathode.

c. High Efficiency Multi-stage Plasma Thruster

This is developed by THALES Electron Devices, Germany, which uses the ion thruster principle. Its propellant consumption is less than 20 % of the chemical system. In this system, low energy neutraliser electrons are confined by magnetic exit cusp and maintain a low plasma potential at the thruster end. A few of these electrons find their way from the neutraliser through the exit cusp of the discharge channel. These electrons are trapped in spirals along their bent magnetic flux lines. The strong magnetic field gradient in the radial direction reflects the electrons like a magnetic mirror. The plasma is achieved by permanent magnets and hence there is no discharge channel erosion.

d. Pulse Plasma Thruster

Pulse Plasma Thruster is the simplest of electric propulsion systems. The Soviet space probe used it in the 1960s.

In this system, an arc is sent through a fuel which turns it into plasma. The plasma is sent through two charged plates energized by capacitors and the plasma gets charged and creates a flow of electrons.

This creates a strong electromagnetic field and exerts a Lorenz Force on the plasma accelerating it out of the exhaust at high velocity. Its operation is similar to the rail-gun in principle.

e. Magneto Plasma Dynamic Thruster

This works on the principle of the Lorenz Force. There is no combustion of fuel. A gaseous material (Xenon, Neon, Argon etc) is ionized and fed into an accelerator chamber, where the magnetic and electric fields are created by a power source. The ionized particles are propelled through the exhaust chamber creating the thrust.

f. Field Emission Electric Propulsion

This is an electrostatic propulsion concept that uses metal ions such as caesium, indium, etc.. A potential difference of several kilovolts is applied between an emitter and accelerator electrodes which accelerates the ions at high velocities. This system is used for precise altitude and direction controls of satellites.

g. Quad Confinement Thruster

Eight electromagnets are arranged to create a convex magnetic field with a central cusp and 4 outer cusps along the periphery. The thrust is produced by the momentum of ions accelerated through a Hall Effect static field.

Conclusion

A brief description of the Maglev, Rail-gun and other propulsion systems is given in this paper. Electromagnetic Propulsion has a wide range of applications including industries, military, and space crafts. Military applications being explored are direct-fire tank guns, long-range artillery, and missile launch. Electromagnetic Propulsion would be the key technology enabler for all-electric naval ships and submarines in the future.

21. VLSI Talent and Issues- India-Specific Overview

Cmde S L Deshmukh

VLSI (Very Large Scale Integrated Circuits) is one of the key element to nourish the domestic electronic hardware industry

With the advent of an accelerated pace of changes in the Information Technology (IT) domain, the emergence of the Internet of Things (IoT), Artificial intelligence (AI) gadgetry, Machine Learning (ML), the need for Very Large Scale Integration (VLSI) in chips manufacturing has become inescapable.

VLSI need specific talents and India is desperately in need of teachers as well as skilled manpower. It is unable to fulfil those requirements as most of the talent gets employed abroad or by MNCs in highly paid jobs. In turn, Indian MSMEs and Start-Ups are starved of the VLSI talent, as they are unable to match the pay scales.

MSMEs and Start-Ups are the backbones of industrial manufacturing in India and it is this sector that supports the requirements of the Indian armed forces and employs a large chunk of youth. India certainly needs to take stock of this dichotomy and institute some remedial measures to resolve the problems.

In view of the above, this article will examine the broad contours of VLSI and its importance, skills needed, current situation in India and some suggested measures.

VLSI and It's Importance

Journey: Transistors, MOSFET, FinFET, VLSI

About 4 decades ago, the world has started witnessing the magic of Transistors. However, due to technical limitations and the size of transistors, a typical number of transistors that could be found in a chip is less than 10,000. For example, a popular Motorola 6800 microprocessor (6.0-μm feature size), developed in the mid-1970s, contained merely 4100 transistors.

However, with the requirements of larger and faster circuits, VLSI started emerging as a new vector. Today, the number of transistors in very-large-scale integration (VLSI) or the super large-scale integration (SLSI) chips could reach 10 billion, with a feature size smaller than 15 nm.

There is not much doubt electronics world has experienced a significant advancement for the past 4 decades or so and this could be attributed to rapidly advancing technology enhancing the performance, power, area, cost and 'time to market' of an integrated circuit (IC) chips.

When transistors were first introduced in the early 1900s, they were actually made of vacuum tubes. These transistors were relatively large in size and cumbersome to be used. In December 1947, however, three physicists working in the AT&T Bell laboratory attained a remarkable breakthrough in their design, changing the perception one used to have on transistors. Dr John Bardeen, Dr Walter Houser Brattain and Dr William Bradford Shockley, Jr., invented the first point-contact semiconductor transistor using germanium.

From these to MOSFET (basically a device that operates like a switch or an amplifier in electronic circuits) to FinFET (with sizes reducing to 22 nm) and now to VLSI (sizes below 15 nm)—it has been an amazing IT journey. (Fig 21.1)

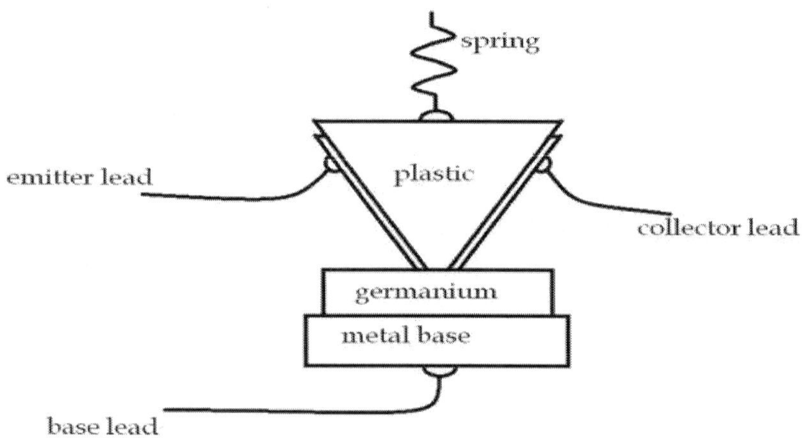

Fig: 21.1- An early model of the point contact transistor. Image Courtesy: intechopen

VLSI Design Flow

Generally, the design process of the chip involves three stages namely the

- behavioural,
- logic circuit and
- layout representations.

At each stage, verification is to be performed at the end before proceeding to the next IC fabrication and IC packaging. Hence, it is common to have repetitions and iterations in the processes. The requisite stages are: -

a. **Behavioural Representation**: At this stage, it is important to specify the functionalities of the device and how it is going to communicate with the exterior. A hardware description language (HDL) such as Verilog HDL or VHDL is used to define the behaviour of the device.

b. **Logic Circuit Representation**: After the HDL codes are successfully simulated, functional blocks from standard cell libraries are used to synthesize the behavioural representation of the design into a logic circuit representation.

c. **Layout Representation**: At the final stage, the physical layout of the design is created. The process starts with floor planning which defines the core and routing areas of the chip. In order to optimize the design, the building blocks are arranged and orientated at their best locations. This process is known as placement. Once this is completed, a routing process is performed to interconnect the building blocks.

d. **Post Layout Representation** IC Fabrication and IC Packaging is done, after which it is ready to be released to the market.

(Sources: Tlelo-Cuautle, 2012 and Yeap and Nisar, 2016)

Importance of VLSI Architecture

The demand and growing sophistication of applications have been continuously pushing the design and manufacturing of integrated circuits and electronic systems to unimaginable levels of complexity. However, this push has also triggered an unprecedented variety of uses. As a consequence of increasing complexity, manufacturers are not only building specific product s but also a wider range of special-purpose systems. This technological ability has become a testament to the growing mastery of both integrated circuit manufacturing and design at one end and increasing demands of customers which test the limits of design and manufacturing at the other. The ability to execute Very Large-Scale Integration (VLSI) has allowed the manufacturers to build systems with a very high number of transistors, enhancing the computing power for solving problems (informIT, 2009).

It has been observed that this technology is quite ideally suited to the ever-increasing demand for complex electronic devices and systems. In addition to requirements for miniaturization, portability, performance, and reliability, and functionality, VLSI technology will continue to drive electronics advancement. For example, the design/manufacture of the PCB depicted in Fig:21.2, with numerous semiconductors, would not be feasible without VLSI technology (Cadence PCB Solutions, ND).

Fig: 21. 2- Complex PCB Design, Image Courtesy: pcb.cadence

VLSI Technology Advantages and Limitations

As any technology would have, VLSI technology too has its advantages and limitations.

Advantages:

Without VLSI technology, it would be impossible to implement, verify, and test the complex, single-chip electronic systems, that are the foundation of the modern-day information technology revolution. The VLSI Technology offers the following distinct advantages: -

a. Reduced size for circuits
b. Increased cost-effectiveness for devices
c. Improved performance in terms of the operating speed of circuits
d. Requires less power than discrete components
e. Higher device reliability
f. Requires less space and promotes miniaturization

Limitations:

VLSI Technology suffers from some limitations too. They are: -

a. Fundamental limitations of design technology.
b. More expensive for device designs.

c. Lack of training infrastructure
d. Limited R and D Resources

(Sources: Bryant et al, 2001, Cadence PCB Solutions, NDa and Kumar, 2017)

Skill Sets Required for VLSI Applications

VLSI field demands high skill set. Some of the important skills which are a pre-requisite for working in VLSI field cover: -

Personal:

a. Problem-solving ability
b. Ability to think out of the box
c. Learning attitude
d. Good listening Skills
e. The ability of working together

Professional:

The VLSI sector is a highly technical field that is totally based on electronics and electrical engineering it demands:

a. Branches conducive for working in the VLSI field are EE (Electrical & Electronics) and EC (Electronics & Communication).
b. Strong capabilities in circuit analysis, analogue electronics, digital electronics, VLSI CMOS, Verilog, etc.
c. Experience in handling projects during engineering related to VLSI or electronics
d. Familiarity with EDA tools that are used in chip design.

(Source: Shidling, 2020)

Current Situation in India

Quality Issues

Experience has shown that the employability of Engineering graduates and their ability to deliver to the VLSI industry expectations, post recruitment has not been up to the mark. It has been observed that it is a problem of both quality and quantity. The quality of VLSI education and the quality of students getting through engineering institutions has been poor. This is because only a few colleges in India have the infrastructure or specific courses related to the VLSI domain. Universities don't have specific courses related to VLSI in their curriculum.

Quantity Issues

It has also been observed that the quantity of VLSI engineers available in India is also quite low. Thus, the VLSI talent is too expensive to hire. The MSME and the StartUp suffer because of this as they cannot afford the high cost of VSLI talent.

Researchers have determined that some institutes in India provide world-class training to VLSI engineers. However, such talent gets immediately hired by companies abroad or MNCs (Intel/ Qualcomm, Samsung, Western Digital etc.) in India at very high pay packages. Thus many good Institutions like IIT Delhi do not get good faculty or Indian Industry, good VLSI engineers. India is thus in a very peculiar bind that it finds very difficult to produce the VLSI talent it needs (Phadnis and John, 2021).

Probable Solutions

The solution to the quality issues is to offer good quality VLSI education with live hands-on projects. The solution to the quantity issues is to offer quality VLSI education in more institutes. To address these issues KLE Tech-IESA-SEER has collaborated for promoting skill set requirement through a set of courses. The courses are designed, delivered and assessed by in-house and industry-expert to build competence. The success story is the extensive industrial experience, internship opportunity and job in VLSI core companies.

As per IESA (India Electronics and Semiconductor Association) Indian Government's Special Manpower Development Program (SMDP) is focused on incentivising the moves from chips to system design and is also providing funds to academic institutions. The industry also opined that highly skilled industry professionals need to be spared to share their expertise with the students in various academic institutions (Phadnis and John, 2021a).

But such efforts are still inadequate to meet India's requirements and lot more needs to be done if India wants to remain a global IT powerhouse.

Conclusion and Suggestions

Chips are becoming core to everything around us today and VLSI is the heart of today's technology revolution. India just cannot afford to lag behind in this field. To become capable and remain relevant in VLSI game India needs to put some measures in place, that too on a fast-track mode. Such measures may cover: -

a. Creation of more quality institutions that will teach curriculum in Electronics and VLSI.

b. Make provision for advanced topics related to VLSI in the curriculum.

c. Teach basics of VLSI at 10+2 level.

d. Create a pool of VLSI talent which could be shared between the industry and the academic institutions.

e. Incentivise industry to gear up for high end Chip fabrication, thus creating more job opportunities and in turn retaining the talent.

Finally, it can be said that India needs to acts fast in this Chips business, before the chips really go down.

Jai Hind

22. Hypersonic Weapons - A Boon for India's Future Defence Capabilities

Mohan Babu

On September 7th, 2020 India test-fired its first Hypersonic Technology Demonstrator Vehicle (HSTDV) from the APJ Abdul Kalam testing range (in the Wheeler Island) in Odisha. By doing so India became the fourth country in the world after the USA, Russia and China to develop and test hypersonic technology. The Defence Research and Development Organisation (DRDO) which developed the HSTDV called the demonstration successful in its press release as critical technologies such as 'aerodynamic configuration for supersonic manoeuvres, scram jet propulsion, etc' were proven. This comes at a time when Prime Minister Narendra Modi has been positing the slogan 'Atmanirbhar Bharat' (Self-Reliant India) at the crux of his speech in every possible platform. The indigenously developed technology is not just a first of its kind for India but is a platform to develop much more sophisticated weapon systems that are bound to boost India's defence capabilities.

Fig 22.1 PC : Asia Financial

Hypersonic Technology

Hypersonic refers to aircraft, missiles, rockets and spacecraft that can travel through the Earth's atmosphere between the speeds of Mach 5 and Mach 10 (Fig 22.1). Hypersonic platforms will be the centrepiece of 21st-century warfare as they are considered to be far deadlier than the existing weapon systems. Hypersonic weapons - are designed to withstand high temperatures and constitute scram-jet propulsion and sophisticated electronics for sensors, communications, guidance and applications in different terrains. Hypersonic weapons increase the accuracy, precision and manoeuvrability of defence operations and are a multi-fold capability amplifier in the modern age of warfare.

Where Other Powers Stand

The USA, in March 2020 tested an unarmed hypersonic missile (Common-Hypersonic Glide Body) successfully. Lt Gen Neil Thurgood who is overseeing Pentagon's Department of Hypersonics, Directed Energy, Space and Rapid Acquisition is quoted as saying that in the days to come, the pace of the program is bound to increase. The US Army aims to add a mobile-land based capability to its arsenal by 2023. The US Navy and the US Army are trying to build a hypersonic industrial base by leading the design and production development respectively. The US Department of Defence (DoD) has requested 3.2 million USD for the fiscal year 2021 solely to boost the research and development of Hypersonic weapons. As per a study conducted by the Institute for Defence Analyses, USA had 48 critical hypersonic test facilities and mobile assets in 2014.There are multiple other facilities in different US Universities, Norway, Australia and so on. In March 2020, the DoD had even set up a hypersonic war room to assess the status of US Industrial base for Hypersonic Weapons. There has been an enormous focus on perfecting the accuracy to increase lethality. The reason for this aggressive pursuit can be attributed to the fact that Russia and China have entered the hypersonic fray and this has pushed the arms race a step further.

Though the USA tested a prototype hypersonic missile in October 2017, Russia by launching the 'Avangard' hypersonic missile in December 2019, became the first country to possess an operable hypersonic weapon. The missile which was launched from the Dombarovskiy missile base in the Urals is claimed to be more than 20 times faster than the speed of sound. Russian President Putin claimed that the development of Avangard was a response to the USA's missile defence system that neutralises Russia's nuclear deterrent. Apart from Avangard, Russia is developing the 3M22 Zircon which is a ship-launched hypersonic cruise missile that is capable of travelling at speeds of between Mach 6 and Mach 8. Though it is tough to identify the credibility of 'Avangard' being inducted into service, the situation definitely adds more potency to the nuclear arms race. Russia houses its hypersonic wind tunnel testing facility at the Institute of Zhukovsky and Khristianovich Institute of Theoretical and Applied Mechanics, Novosibirsk. Hypersonic testing happens at Dombarovskiy Air Base, Baykonur Cosmodrome and Kura Range. The Russian Navy has been converting old warships into Hypersonic delivery platforms thereby making up for the shortfall in budgetary allocation (The actual budgetary allocation is not known) as well as general weakness.

China for its part has been involved in developing hypersonic technology since 2014. In the National Day Parade on October 01, 2019, China showcased the Dong Feng-17 Hypersonic glide-boost missile. DF-17's two-fold speciality is that it is capable of cruising at lower altitudes that makes it difficult to track and is highly accurate. Apart from DF-17, China is currently testing of the wave rider hypersonic missile- Xingkong-2. The Xingkong-2 as claimed by China is to counter the adversary's anti-missile defence system with high speed and manoeuvrability. China is said to have conducted more hypersonic tests than the US and houses an efficient research and development ecosystem dedicated to hypersonic weapons. China also has set up multiple hypersonic wind tunnels and is said to have tested the hypersonic weapons at the Jiuaquan Satellite Launch Centre. As China has shown to the world, its defence programmes focus on high rates of production via efficient programmes and policy backing.

Implications for India

India enters the hypersonic race at a juncture where the USA, Russia and China are already looking into developing improvised hypersonic platforms to stretch their capabilities. It is worthy to mention that India is developing the BrahMos-II of BrahMos Aerospace, an Indo-Russian Joint Venture. The missile will use the scramjet technology that is identical to what Zircon has. However, does India really have the capacity to add more such weapons to its arsenal?

We need to take into account two things, to begin with. Firstly, India has to build a conducive design, development and manufacturing ecosystem. At present, India lacks a dedicated Defence Industrial Base (DIB). Though the words 'Atmanirbhar Bharat' stir up a sense of national pride, the practicality of how well hypersonic missile development could blend as a self-reliant endeavour is a question for policymakers to ponder with. Ironically, the BrahMos-II was tested in Russia as India does not house multiple testing facilities as Russia, USA or China does.

Secondly, the economic impact of the same would be far-reaching. As per the 2020-2021 Defence Budget, only 6% has been allocated for the DRDO. Though the share of the Defence budget has increased 9% over the previous budget, the expense meant for modernisation may not bear fruits. The COVID-19 pandemic too has inflicted a major dent to India's aspirations vis-a-vis the future budgets. The forthcoming budget(s) may not allocate much for defence modernisation either. The major focus will be on covering up for the development rhetoric on other sectors such as education and health.

With that being said, the HSTDV test comes at a time where the tension between India and China has been increasing across the Line of Actual Control (LAC). The test can be viewed as a clear message sent to the Chinese establishment that India is gearing up for the future. Further, in the lines of Amb Sujan Shinoy's comment, India must work on improving the depth and quality of technology transfer deals with the US and focus on not just buying items off the shelf but on importing sophisticated defence technologies. The Indian policymakers too need to work on putting domestic start-ups and MSMEs to better use, if India was to create an indigenous ecosystem for the Research, Development and manufacturing of futuristic defence technologies. With the help of a holistic policy backing, well-planned technology transfer and the right infrastructure, India can accentuate its efforts towards creating a hypersonic arsenal.

23. Swarm Technology in Drones - Towards Self-reliance

Dr Apoorva Joshi

Autonomous systems, especially unmanned aerial vehicles, have seen engagements ranging from covert surveillance operations to active war zone operations in recent times. With technological developments in computation modules and communication systems, we are quickly moving towards the notion of networked autonomous agents, colloquially also known as swarming. (Fig 23.1)

Fig 23. 1 PC :SP

Swarming as a strategy in military affairs is quite ancient, but with advances in technology, it is possible to build autonomous agents to mimic such behaviour. Due to the relative recency in the technological breakthroughs that enable swarming, India stands a great chance to develop self-reliance in this domain and use it to her advantage. It is therefore essential for our security agencies and engineers to collaborate in achieving this goal. This article outlines the advantages that swarming, or cooperative behaviour offers, a few examples of the sort of work that is being done by Indian academia and offers some personal views on how to move ahead to achieve self-reliance.

Swarming as a military doctrine and the role that intelligent agents will play in future conflicts has been well studied in the US. Similar studies, for example to understand how swarming could be useful in the Indian context by military experts, would serve as a guideline to engineers in their development efforts. It is also prudent to have a thorough understanding of our neighbours' developments in this domain. On the technical front, research in swarming took off with Reynolds' description of the motion of flocks of birds, or herds of animals, or schools of fish as computer animations. Since then, computer scientists and control theorists have been working on algorithms to achieve cooperation between artificial agents. A branch of this study is known as multi-agent systems (MAS). This branch draws from knowledge in graph theory, control theory and optimization to study and develop algorithms for cooperative behaviour.

Multi-agent systems (MAS) are capable of performing various tasks. These tasks can be categorized into the following classes:

Spatial assembly: Agents coordinate to achieve specific spatial configurations, but have negligible interaction with the environment. These tasks can be subdivided into:

- Aggregation: agents converge onto one location
- Pattern formation: agents arrange themselves into formations
- Coverage: agents cover an area of interest

Collective exploration: Agents interact with the environment but have minimal interactions with each other. These tasks can be subdivided into:

- Area exploration: agents explore an area for mapping or surveillance
- Goal searching: agents search for specific targets

Cooperative decision making: Agents coordinate between themselves and interact with the environment to achieve complex tasks. These tasks can be subdivided into:

- Task allocation: tasks are distributed amongst agents based on various parameters
- Collective transport: agents coordinate to transport heavy payloads
- Motion planning: agents collaborate to find paths in cluttered environments
- Distributed estimation: the state of one or multiple targets can be estimated using data from multiple agents.

Military missions are typically designed over several phases, each comprising tactics and plays that various units perform. The aforementioned tasks that the

MAS can perform, need to be embedded into these military tactics and plays. This embedding is critical to leverage the true power of multi-agent systems. Hence, a strong open collaboration with our internal security forces is essential. Inputs from officers with ground experience would help in designing practical missions, with MAS providing tactical advantages.

In recent years, a lot of effort has been put into realizing state-of-the-art multi-agent systems in India. Several test beds have been designed to demonstrate cooperative behaviour through various tasks. A test bed was created to demonstrate the task of aggregation in outdoor environments. The agents communicated with each other using a real-time communication protocol and reached consensus regarding the location of rendezvous, without centralized command or control. Novel algorithms to demonstrate formation flight and rogue agent capture in minimum time were also tested. Various demonstrations of the task of coverage have been covered. As an extension of this work, we are now capable of demonstrating complicated missions wherein a group of agents take off from a home location and navigate to an area of interest to set up a surveillance network. The agents optimally cover this area of interest and also perform the task of goal searching. Once the goal/target is found, the agents form patterns around the target to gather more intelligence and relay it back to central command for further action.

These demonstrations have enabled us to understand areas that need further work. One critical area, which needs collaboration with security forces is that of human-swarm interaction. MAS operates on high-level commands from humans and generate a lot of sensory data. This data is analysed by a central command centre. The data is also useful for system health monitoring and taking decisions on a tactical level. Development of information flows and interfaces could be made end-user ready with their inputs at the design and demonstration stage. On the technical side, mission composability and provability of safe operations is a challenge we are working on. A multi-agent system is a system of systems. Hence stability and performance guarantees need to be ensured for successful operation.

As we move towards self-reliance in technology for swarms, it is essential that engineers and security forces collaborate. Together, technology demonstrators need to be designed based on specific use cases, current technological limitations and financial constraints. One good step in this direction was the recent Meher Baba challenge by the IAF. More such nuanced demonstrations need to be planned and executed.

A few startups are doing good work in this area. Mentorship from the security experts would help us design better systems. As an engineer, I look forward to interacting with our security agencies and welcome constructive feedback for achieving this common goal for our nation.

24. AI Technology in the Military Transformation of Future Warfare

Prof Amit Das and Manish K Jha

Artificial Intelligence is strongly influencing each domain of life. Technology always decides the pace of society and it redefines the social parameters with unique outputs. The incarnation of AI is motivating global powers to prepare themselves to control and manoeuvre advanced technologies to establish dominance in power-play. Artificial Intelligence is the new paradigm of power in between the superpowers. Technology is an important factor that determines the effective power of modern military warfare. It enables the military to encounter complex challenges in effective and innovative methods and could be a strong component for future warfares. The global military institutions and countries are trying to identify the areas where machine intelligence could be plug-in with the regular military operations.

The essence of modern warfare is more complex due to an adequate number of micro variables. Change in any variable could create an exponential impact on the war. The induction of AI is converting the war from specialized-mechanized war to intelligent-robotic-digitized war-fare. The global powers are preparing their military and establishments to take leverage of modern intelligent technologies to optimize the war results. The establishment of PLASSF (People's Liberation Army Strategic Support Force) by the Xi-Jinping Government in 2015 is showcasing the Chines seriousness about the induction of technology in military and warfare. To challenge American supremacy and for the absolute development in the Military-AI technologies, the Chinese policymakers released its 10th Defence White Paper, China's National Defence in the New Era roadmap for the complete AI-ecosystem for the Chinese Army.

Artificial Intelligence could help to enhance the multi-layer capabilities of the military forces to handle various undefined war situations or hostile environments. AI provides the capability of rapid decision making in an information-dense environment and also in information sparse situations.

For the military the AI could be encapsulated under the following heads in a phased manner: -

Phase 1: Gradual development of different AI techniques for the Military.

Phase 2: Timely deployment of AI techniques for armed forces functional applications.

Phase 3: Constant discovery of applications of AI techniques for the military.

Phase 4: Fabrication of future roadmap for the military.

The integration of AI with military regular operations could upgrade the logistics, administration, maintenance, training, personal management and routine activities or exercises. It could reduce the institutional workload and free up the warriors for the core functions. AI could handle the OODA (Observe-Orient-Decide-Act) loop faster, create combat intelligent clouds with secure gateways. The AI could upgrade the Command-and-Control capabilities of armed forces with a resilient approach. The Military-AI-Ecosystem could support the higher formations to design and deploy more effective and efficient battle plans for better control on operations with sharper and deep insights. The new intelligent technologies could speed up the capabilities of decision making, helps higher officials to generate more offensive or defensive decisions during wars or combats. AI could accelerate the system for the three sixty-degree analyses of the environment for better decision making with the strong feature of an autonomous system.

The combat skills of the future military could be enhanced under the following heads:

- AI-based smart logistics with more integrated actions
- AI-based transportation system for each node of the establishment.
- AI- Enabled target recognition system for the Naval, Air or Army.
- Unmanned Combat Aerial Vehicle
- Unmanned Intelligent Ground Vehicle
- AI-Enabled deep analysis of integrated warfare theaters (Land, Naval and Air)
- Cyber Security
- Cyber Warfare
- Robotic battle fields
- Advanced war simulators
- AI-based War games for the training of the forces
- Predictive and sequential analysis of threats and situations
- Use of AI techniques for military data processing and analysis.
- AI based Missile Guided System
- AI-based Autonomous weapon system

In modern warfare extensive strategic intelligence is required with more sophisticated integration of technological components to deals with the situational requirements of war theatres. War-Zones are one of the areas where each discrete event is overloaded with a high volume of integrated data. AI could create more taxonomies of events from the available data sets. Wars drove by the information; AI may provide or recommend valuable options to the commanders or may be able to provide the best options which the human brain could provide.

The global military powers are smartly working towards modelling a common platform to handle the context-based challenges from seabeds to space using the convergence of disruptive technologies combined with the different tools of AI. This entire processing is creating the military wars more knowledge-based rather than quantity based- a radical shift from attrition and destruction to one of the effects and outcomes.

The fusion of old war skills with AI technology is approaching towards news doctrinal concept of war that is based on rapid and accurate decisions, deployments and destruction of the adversary's ability and will to fight and not merely targeting its armament and arsenals. Physical Bravery on the battlefield as we know it has now shifted to courage in the cyberspace of digitized warfare.

AI is the next-generation weapon required to transform how the armed forces operate, train and fight from the barracks to the trenches. AI-Based models are necessary for each country to demystify the hidden war behaviour of the enemy country. The accurate decisions with AI could create an exponential effect on the conduct and outcome of the war.

It may also be mentioned that it is possible to tweak existing algorithms from the commercial space and find use cases of the same for military applications. This requires a larger understanding of the technology and a deeper understanding of the entire design of battle. A silo-based approach would be highly expensive, time-consuming and only duplicate algorithms that are already residing in other domains as solve problems. AI by themselves would not provide the complete solution and the requisite underlays of hardware and the overlays of networks and systems is a necessity.

Machine learning and deep learning may be used to decode the unsupervised learning between the hidden nodes of the war.

The operational knowledge AI is competent to enhance the operational capabilities of submarines on sea-beds. The cognitive quality of AI may help submarines to sense the qualitative observations of the environment for reacting more sophisticated approach. International maritime always creates a high volume of data from sea-profiling to ship movement. The hidden strategic information from those data could be extracted with the help of AI for the smart maritime strategy. The likelihood of success may be increased by the association of different maritime domain knowledge through the integrated nature of AI technology.

The emergent challenges always occur in Air-Warfare and absolute response is required to face such issues. The AI-based situational responses may provide more accurate context to our aircraft. Effective encapsulation of AI with Human Intelligence may create more accurate air attacks from fighter planes and choppers.

The fusion of AI with War-Strategy may generate deep strategic insights for the commanders and may help countries reduce war losses due to its predictive and subjective nature and achieve objectives through outcome-driven engagements.

25. Deepfakes And Shallowfakes

Cmde BR Prakash

In an era where social media content zips across the internet at the speed of light, ideas, words and phrases are generated at a staggering pace, leaving the uninitiated confounded. Therefore, I am not sure if many of us have heard the new additions to the English lexicon - deepfakes and shallowfakes, let alone understand what they mean. They can change the narratives and could affect both internal as well as external security of a nation.

Most of us are familiar with the deliberate spread of misinformation or partisan content, on social media, coined 'fake news', which is influencing political and social landscapes across the globe. The fake news devoid of realistic images or videos does not create the intended impact, as the old English adage says "a picture is worth a thousand words". Until recently, a professional video editor with his team along with sophisticated video editing tools was essential to alter or recreate images. Techniques such as morphing using Photoshop is passé as it can easily discernible to even casual scrutiny. This limited the spread of authentic-looking fake images. However, in the last two years, technological advances and the ubiquitous internet have enabled the average John Doe to swiftly create and disseminate high quality tampered video, aided by an ever-growing social media.

"Shallowfakes" have been around for a while and refer to the numerous (tens of thousands of videos) circulated with malicious intent worldwide, which are not crafted with sophisticated AI, but often simply recycled, staged or re-edited and relabelled content uploaded on the net. It may be as simple as mislabelling content to discredit someone or spread false information. Shallowfakes have been in use in recent times with devastating effect as shown by the recent example of the doctored video of US House Speaker Nancy Pelosi that went viral and was retweeted by President Donald Trump.

It was only in 2017 that the world woke up to "deepfakes" when it was used as a moniker by a Reddit user. Deepfake is a portmanteau of "deep learning" and "fake". It started with an anonymous Reddit user posting digitally altered pornographic videos using machine-learning technology. While the user was banned by Reddit, it spurred a wave of copycats on other platforms. Experts believe there are now about 10,000 deepfake videos circulating online, and the number is growing.

The use of this machine learning technique hitherto was mostly limited to the AI research community in universities and it was only when the Reddit user started using Generative Adversarial Networks (GANs), that the common man became aware of its application to video and images. He was building GANs using TensorFlow, Google's free open-source machine learning software, to superimpose celebrities' faces on the bodies of women in pornographic movies.

However, for the people who think this is Geek (essentially anybody without a PhD in AI), it is a machine learning technique, invented by a graduate student, Ian Goodfellow, in 2014 as a method to algorithmically generate new types of data out of existing data sets. GAN is a class of machine learning systems where two neural networks contesting with each other in a game (in the sense of game theory, often but not always in the form of a zero-sum game). Given a training set, this technique learns to generate new data with the same statistics as the training set. Photo images are readily available online. In 2017, it was estimated that 1,000 selfies are uploaded to Instagram every second. The more pictures of the target, the more realistic the deep fake. GANs can also be used to generate new audio from existing audio, or new text from an existing text – it is a multi-use technology.

In plain English, in deepfake technology, GANs are trained to replicate patterns, such as the face of a person, which gradually improves the realism of the synthetically generated faces. Basically, it works like a cat-and-mouse game between two neural networks. One network, called "the generator," is producing the fake video based on training data (real images), and the other network, "the discriminator," is trying to distinguish between the real images and the fake video. This iterative process continues until the generator is able to fool the discriminator into thinking that the footage is real.

This was logically taken to the next level by the creator of the videos who released FakeApp, an easy-to-use platform for making forged media. The free software effectively democratized the power of GANs. Now, anyone with access to the internet and pictures of a person's face could generate their own deep fake. The quality of the videos produced by the software beats the current state of the art face recognition systems based on VGG and Facenet neural networks, with 85.62% and 95.00% false acceptance rates (on high-quality versions) respectively.

On May 19, researchers at the Samsung AI Center in Moscow developed a way to create "living portraits" from a very small dataset—as few as one photograph, in some of their models. This, in a way, is a leap beyond what even deepfakes and other algorithms using generative adversarial networks can accomplish. Instead of teaching the algorithm to paste one face onto another using a catalogue of expressions from one person, they use the facial features that are common across most humans to then puppeteer a new face. The details of the process are based on the paper, "Few-Shot Adversarial Learning of Realistic Neural Talking Head Models".

While altering pornographic content does not affect the public at large, however, in the future, deep fakes could be exploited by purveyors of "fake news" to create digital wildfires. There is always the danger of our networked information environment interacting in toxic ways with our cognitive biases based on fake news. Deep fakes will exacerbate this problem significantly. Anyone with access to this technology – from state-sanctioned propagandists to trolls – would be able to skew information, manipulate beliefs, and in so doing, push ideologically opposed online communities deeper into their own subjective realities.

To counter the growing stream of fake news, misinformation and deepfakes are tough as it is hard to keep up with. Relying on forensic detection alone to combat deep fakes is becoming less viable, due to the rate at which machine learning techniques can circumvent them. Work is in progress to develop forensic technology to identify digital forgeries, with new detection methods to counteract the spread of deep fakes. Techniques to identify subtle changes of colour that occur in the face as blood is pumped in and out are being explored, as the signal is so minute that the machine learning software is unable to pick it up – at least for now.

So, there is hope that in the future, that deepfakes could be countered using the same AI, which helped to created it.

26. 'Smart Ship' Construction Takes Roots in India

Dr Vijay Sakhuja

The Indian shipbuilding industry has taken 'baby steps' into the world of autonomous vessels. Asko Maritime AS, a subsidiary of the group of Norges Gruppen ASA, Norway, placed orders with Cochin Shipyard Limited (CSL) to build two emission-free electrical-powered autonomous vessels. The 67-metre-long vessel is designed by Naval Dynamics Norway and Kongsberg Maritime systems and the detailed engineering will be carried out by the CSL. It would carry 16 trailers onboard and operate in Oslo fjords.

There are at least four important reasons for the global move towards building smart vessels; first, the shipping industry seeks to harness Industry 4.0 technologies for enhancing efficiency, harmonize ship operations with the supply chain and reduce downtime through predictive maintenance; second is about reducing pollution from ships which are known to emit enormous amounts of GHG gasses that impact the environment and contribute to climate change; third, is the reduction of personnel on board ships for cost-cutting and using their living spaces for cargo; and fourth, reduce accidents given that nearly 70 to 80 percent of ship accidents at sea are a result of human error.

In the above context, autonomous vessels are making a debut in the global maritime ecosystem and over 2000 autonomous and semi-autonomous vessels could be operating by 2025. The market trends for autonomous ships are indeed very encouraging and this segment is "estimated to be USD 6.1 billion in 2018 and is projected to reach USD 13.8 billion by 2030, at a CAGR of 7.00% from 2018 to 2030."

A number of autonomous ship projects are currently underway; for instance, *Kongsberg Maritime,* a Norwegian technology enterprise is building *Yara Birkeland,* an "autonomous electric-powered vessel", capable of carrying 100 to 150 shipping containers. The European Commission has funded collaborative project MUNIN (Maritime Unmanned Navigation through Intelligence in Networks) that features automated on-board decision systems but controlled by a remote operator in a shore side control station."

In Asia, Japan is leading in autonomous ship technology development and a consortium of shipping and engineering companies, research institutes and laboratories were shortlisted by Japan's Ministry of Land, Infrastructure, Transportation and Tourism to develop a technological concept for autonomous ocean transport system. (Fig 26.1) The project, based on Industry 4.0 technologies, is estimated to cost "tens of billions of yen, or hundreds of millions of dollars, at a minimum".

Fig 26.1 PC: Siemens

In 2020, China announced steel cutting for its first autonomous containership named Zhi Fei to be constructed at Qingdao shipyard. These 5,000 tons vessels can carry up to 300 TEUs and is being fitted with intelligent navigation systems. It would have electric propulsion which would reduce noise and its advanced systems to reduce NOx, SOx and CO2 gasses.

The international technology conglomerates too are supporting smart ship production. The IBM is engaged in the development of autonomous vessel called 'Mayflower Autonomous Ship (MAS)' which is being equipped with IBM's Power AI Vision technology and an IBM Deep Learning-powered collision avoidance system to maintain autonomous safety of navigation. Similarly, Rolls-Royce is among the pioneers in autonomous ship technology, and its €6.6 million project -Advanced Autonomous Waterborne Applications Initiative (AAWA) - is supported by the Finnish Funding Agency for Technology and Innovation to examine the future of autonomous ships.

The MASS technology is in its infancy and is expected to improve in the coming future. However, the major challenge is human-resource who would need to be educated and trained for adoption and assimilation of new technologies for which they must develop specialist skills for MASS operations both at sea and ashore. This would entail significant investment in training infrastructure, bridging the digital education divide, and research for this new technological age. There will also be challenges on account of existing workers' skills who would require to upgrade on a continuing basis, as also for those workers being displaced or having their jobs eliminated.

Technological advancements have been the feature of the Cochin Shipyard Limited (CSL). Since its incorporation in 1972 as a fully owned Government of India company, the shipyard has built large merchant vessels and military platforms such as aircraft carriers; it has also excelled in the ship repair business. It has commercial linkages with foreign shipyards and the most recent strategic business partnership is with M/s. Fincantieri, one of the world's largest shipbuilding groups. Their memorandum of understanding envisages focus on indigenization in shipbuilding for India in support of the 'Atmanirbhar Bharat' and 'Make in India' vision of Indian government.

The Cochin Shipyard Limited has now made a very promising beginning in the smart ship segment and is therefore reasonably primed to attract many other international partners to build 'smart vessels'. This should trigger interest among Indian technology and product developers such as the Kochi based Maker Village and concept developer MSME such as DRaS, to explore Industry 4.0 technologies for 'smart vessels'. This would also help India ride the current wave of technology and not being left behind in the future shipping environment. Asian shipbuilding giants such as Japan, Korea, China and Singapore are the leading countries in shipbuilding as also in Industry 4.0 technologies and the gap with them is quickly widening.

27. Smart Couture: Customized Military Clothing

Dr Vijay Sakhuja

Smart couture or smart uniforms are going to be an important wearable for soldiers in the coming decade.

The Indian and Chinese armies are 'all set' for a long haul in the snowcapped Himalayan mountains after their recent standoff in the Ladakh sector. They are preparing to endure the harsh weather conditions given that heavy snowfall will start soon; the temperature would drop to minus 50 degrees Celsius, and wind velocity of 40 kilometres per hour will make the area most inhospitable. Soldiers on both sides are being equipped with 'smart' gears; the PLA has placed orders for "smart warm clothing made of graphene", a revolutionary form of carbon, for which physicists Andra Geim and Konstantine Novoselov were awarded the Nobel Prize in 2010; and the Indian Army has set up "smart camps" and provided for "11,000 sets of special clothes recently taken from the US" among other high altitude essential materials for use by its soldiers. Meanwhile, dialogue and communications through the diplomatic and military channels continue with both sides taking hard positions on troop withdrawals.

The technical requirements of smart couture and Integrated Military Fabrics and Garments (SIMFG) i.e. combat uniform/field uniform/battledress, footwear, gloves, headgear, balaclavas, jacket windcheater and accessories such as carry packs is quite unique. This necessitates a clear understanding of the environment in which they operate. There are at least six requirements for a SIMFG.

First, it should be light and comfortable so that the combatant can move unhindered while performing his duties. In this context, the clothing should be both 'smart and intelligent' to read the surrounding temperature as also cool/warm the soldier's body through ventilation/heating mechanisms (natural or mechanical) including moisture management. (Fig 27.1)

Second, SIMFG should generate the necessary power requirements for various operations. This can be obtained through embedded piezoelectric cells, power generating temperature differential devices or by capturing thermal energy produced by the human body movements.

Fig 27.1 PC: CNET

Third, SIMFG should also be able to provide Chameleonic camouflage to the soldier through specific patterns across topographies by changing its colour and disruptive patterns. For instance, in jungle warfare, military fatigues are olive green in colour; it is brown and similar shades for desert clothing and white in the mountains. It is useful to mention that "patterns of digital camouflage, at a certain distance, merge faster with the environment".

Fourth is about linking to other 'connected clothing' and devices. It should be blue-tooth enabled so that data can be viewed in real-time on the companion/controller's smartphone app or other external devices to send alerts through notifications or text messages. An invisible biometric sensor would be an added advantage.

Fifth, the SIMFG should be able to integrate flexible displays. A number of multiscreen-foldable smart devices are now available in the market and the SIMFG would be able to fully integrate these.

Sixth, the smart fabric should be highly hygienic, water-resistant, and should not require frequent washing. It should also be crafted aesthetically. Seventh is about sustainability, a mantra which is resonating across the militaries. The SIMFG should be powered by renewables and designed for re-use, re-purpose and recycle.

As far as headgear is concerned, these can be woven/stitched and embedded with sensors to detect temperature, monitor air quality and warn of UV rays. The footwear can be a good place to store batteries and a USB connection can facilitate charging and power distribution through the SIMFG by using electrical conductive yarn thereby "getting rid of multiple batteries and cables in the uniform used to power different equipment."

These are indeed unique requirements and certainly attract challenges; first is about the cost of the SIMFG which is the key to its production and adoption have given that militaries are constrained by both budgets and limited requirements of numbers. The business model must clearly justify the added value that compensates the investment in SIMFG.

It is useful to note that the textile and fashion industry is not new to smart fabrics, given that the "global smart fabrics market witnessed 4.1 million units' shipments in 2019, and it is expected to reach a shipment value of 8. 51 million units by 2025, registering a CAGR of 14. 1% over the forecast period (2020 – 2025)". In particular, the military segment of the global smart couture /textiles market was expected to grow at a CAGR of close to 10% between 2016 and 2020.

The second challenge is finding an appropriate technology, an effective design and architecture that combines new materials and technologies with adjustable properties. SIMFG is evolving rapidly and new technologies are being integrated to give it 'Hyper stealth'. For instance, 'Quantum Stealth' material is being developed that can "remove not only visual, infrared (night vision) and thermal signatures but also the target's shadow". Similarly, Nanotechnology is being harnessed to "conceal the visibility of a person even in ultraviolet and infra-red rays from a particular distance"; Furthermore, it can also "arouse the muscle power, which will give the soldier more strength in doing tough jobs". Biomimetic can be put to use to create Chameleonic camouflage by "creating intelligent surfaces" in which the SIMFG identifies its surroundings and changes colour.

Finally, militaries across the globe are in the throes of Industry 4.0 technological revolution (4IR) and are acquiring everything 'smart' to overwhelm or deter the adversary. The acquisitions are not just limited to 4IR-enabled military hardware, fighting equipment/devices and ammunitions; the soldiers are being draped in 'smart couture' with integrated circuits woven into the garment and sensors embedded and such clothing will soon be an intrinsic part of their 'smart combat equipment'

28. Network Centric Warfare and Emerging Communication Technologies

Cmde Naresh Kumar

Command Control Computers, Communications and Intelligence (C4I) systems for Intelligence, Surveillance and Reconnaissance (ISR) have undergone a sea change with the ever-advancing communication network and power for information processing. With low flying sea-skimming missiles and hypersonic missile threats, the reaction time available to detect track and classify target is very small. It requires automatic processing of the sensor data, multi-sensor data correlation, threat assessment based on the speed, direction to engage the same with the most suitable weapon. The C4I systems are essential to:

- Defend and protect all domains
- Make better, faster decisions
- Access trusted, actionable intelligence in real-time
- Shorten the sensor-to-shooter timeline
- Gain 360° situational awareness
- Execute more successful, efficient missions

The requirement of all three services are different though with Special operation Forces, there is a dire need for interoperability. Indian Navy is a blue water Navy operating an aircraft carrier and has a large number of ships deployed over the Indian ocean and now far east with emerging threat scenario. The Indian army has a very long and hostile border area in the north and western front to defend. Indian Airforce has a vast area of operation and with the missile threat and supersonic aircraft, the ISR operations and launching the attack require split-second decisions. All three services, therefore, require secure communications across long ranges. The information received from a large number of sensors needs to be processed in the Command centres for quick decisions.

Each service over the last three operates have been building the network-centric capabilities, the Indian Navy inducted its first computerised Command and control system onboard ships in the early eighties. The system was linked to all the onboard sensors and weapons through high-speed data bus and Interfaces. The raw radar picture received from radars was processed and the plots and tracks were generated by the video extractors. Multi radar correlation was performed to accurately estimate and track the target position. Based on the speed, angle of arrival and other inputs from Electronic warfare systems, the target threat evaluation was computed for all the Air targets every second and common operating picture was displayed to the operators in the operation room of the ship. All the defensive and offensive actions were performed as per defined warfighting doctrine programmed in the system to engage the targets with the most suitable weapons. The system had the surface warfare, subsurface and air warfare operations controlled by the operational software running in the CMS system computers. The threatening targets could also be passed on Link 11 type of system to the accompanying ships and aircraft in the fleet through UHF, VHF or HF modems connected to the Link controller. The satellite communications were not available for command and control function at that time and the Inmarsat was primarily used for rescue missions at sea.

Navy has made huge progress in the Command and Control and Communication network since then. Every ship is fitted with the state of art command and control system having the much more advanced sensors and weapons. 3 D stabilised phased array radars provide highly accurate target detection and tracking capability using multiple beams steering techniques. A typical ship has about thirty sensors and weapon systems including navigational systems, Gyros, Inertial navigational system, GPS, Navigational and surveillance Radars, Short- and Long-range Guns, Electronic warfare system Active and Passive Sonars, Towed decoy, Chaff launchers, Short- and long-range Torpedoes, Surface to Surface and Surface to Air Missiles, a couple of helicopters carrying Torpedo and or missiles. Managing data from so many systems is humanly impossible and the Combat Management System which is integrated with all the weapons and sensors is the central Command and Control system for all operations, most of them automated or assisted automatic operations to reduce the reaction time.

As the Navy operates in Blue waters far away from its shore the Navy was also the first service to get its own communication satellite for long haul communications. With the Induction of P8I and UAVs, the Command and Control systems have become much more complex with high-speed telemetry links to transfer the critical ISR information in real-time to the ships and aircraft and Command centres for appropriate action. The Navy has been continuously upgrading its Communication networks and the Combat Management systems onboard ships and aircraft. Navy also started its datalink project many years ago and along with CMS, a LINK 11 type of Data Link system and functions were embedded in the CMS to realise seamless communication between the Ships and Aircrafts operating at sea. These systems are now interfaced with the Satellite Communication systems to achieve wide-area connectivity. However, with the emerging technologies, secure communications across the glove remains a challenge with the Cyber Security threat. Navy has therefore launched phase 2 of the Naval Communication network project with the local Indian companies to upgrade its networking capabilities. This network will give the Indian Navy digital defence supremacy at par with the best naval forces in the world. It includes the creation of an independent high-capacity end-to-end communications network, linking multiple Indian naval sites and India-administered islands. It will include setting-up of highly secure data centres and Big Data content delivery networks that are software-defined.

The Joint operations amongst the services have further extended the complexity of the command and control operations with inputs from a large number of systems of the other two services. The operations are over the Global range which can only be covered by the Satellite Communications connecting seamlessly to all fixed and mobile assets.

Naval Data Link Communication Environment

While the Navy was building its command and control system capabilities over the last three decades, both Airforce and Army have also been upgrading their communication and Command centres. To provide a big boost to the operational capability of defence forces, the Cabinet Committee on Security (CCS) has recently given its approval for Army Static Switched Communication Network (ASCON) Phase IV of the Indian Army at an estimated cost of around Rs 7796.39 crore to M/S ITI. This is going to be an upgrade on the existing Asynchronous Transfer Mode Technology to Internet Protocol (IP) / Multi-Protocol Label Switching (MPLS) Technology. Also, Optical Fibre Cable (OFC), Microwave Radio and Satellite will be used for communication. In any operational scenario with almost 80 per cent indigenous content, this system is expected to provide better survivability, responsiveness and high bandwidth. It will enhance the communication coverage of the network closer to IB/LC/LAC. Through this network, the high bandwidth communication will extend to the remote operational areas in the Central and Eastern Sectors. And will also reach to the forward locations in the Western border. This whole project is expected to augment the communication network of the Indian Army in the sensitive forward operational areas (Fig 28.1).

Airforce has also implemented its Integrated Air Command and Control System (IACCS) for controlling and monitoring of air operations by Air Force. The information-sharing involves sharing of the critical data through dedicated links among Navy, Army and Civil Radar network also. The IACCS system receives data from different types of homogeneous/ heterogeneous radars (2-D or 3-D), generate reports from mobile observation posts and integrates other data elements from various other Air Force bases or Civilian agencies viz Air Traffic Control, Air Force Movement Liaison Unit including airborne AWACS to create a real-time comprehensive air situation picture at Command & Control centre. A large VoIP (Voice over Internet Protocol) layer with stringent quality of service enforcement facilitates robust, high-quality voice, video and conferencing solutions, an automated command and control system for Air Defence (AD) operations, ride the AFNET backbone integrating all ground-based and airborne sensors, AD weapon systems and C2 nodes. All major formations and static establishments have been linked through a secure Wide Area Network (WAN) and are accessible through data communication lines. The Indian Air Force has already established Command and Control nodes using AFNET backbone. The primary objective to deploy such an integrated solution derived from all airborne and ground-based civilian and military radars around the country is to ensure any intrusion by a hostile aircraft, helicopter, drone or micro-light can be detected and tackled as soon as it takes place. Indian Air Force is also using ISRO Satellite Centre, GSAT-7A similar to Indian navy's GSAT-7 which enables IAF to interlink different ground radar stations, ground airbase and Airborne early warning and control AWACS.

The Joint operations amongst the services have further extended the complexity of the command and control operations with inputs from a large number of systems of the other two services and all three services have a long way to go to achieve seamless connectivity and joint operations with ever-changing threats, communication technology using satellite and space communications across the length and breadth of the country and its island territories and far beyond where these Forces are required to operate.

Satellites have been in the inventory of modern militaries and used for navigation, accurate delivery of ordnance over long distances, and Intelligence, Surveillance and Reconnaissance (ISR) tasks. The two Gulf Wars and the global war on terror demonstrated that satellites were game changers and facilitated accurate targeting of terrorists and their hideouts with little collateral damage. SpaceX has recently added 60 new satellites to the Starlink internet constellation, an internet service project which aims to provide broadband services across the globe and has plans to launch nearly 12,000 satellites into orbit to provide high-speed broadband internet at locations where access is "unreliable, expensive, or completely unavailable. SpaceX has received orders from the US Space Development Agency (SDA) for satellites that can track and provide early warnings of hypersonic missile launches. The satellites are part of the SDA's Tracking Layer which will work in conjunction with the proposed Transport Layer (constellation of between 300 and 500 satellites) and will provide "low-latency military data and connectivity worldwide" to military assets.

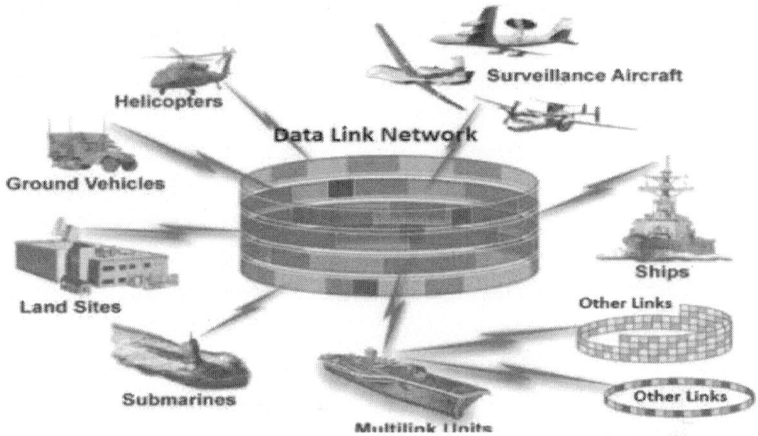

Fig 28. 1 PC: FICCI Events

The Basic Exchange and Communication agreement (BECA) recently signed with US will help India get real-time access to American geospatial intelligence that will enhance the accuracy of automated systems and weapons like missiles and armed drones. Through the sharing of information on maps and satellite images, it will help India access topographical and aeronautical data, and advanced products that will aid in navigation and targeting. BECA will provide Indian military systems with a high-quality GPS to navigate missiles with real-time intelligence to precisely target the adversary.

The future ISR shall be driven by the environment" driven by the Fourth Industrial Revolution (4IR) technologies that are smart and intelligent, use predictive-cognitive tools and algorithms, and drive autonomous, unmanned and remote-controlled platforms, robots and machines. Some of the frontline technologies of 4IR are Artificial Intelligence (AI), Machine Learning (ML), Big Data, cloud computing, Augmented Reality (AR), Quantum Computing, Cognitive Computing (CC) and Internet of Things (IoT) are gathering momentum and finding use in supporting ISR operations. These operations therefore are highly complex and Technology driven and India has to be self-reliant in these areas. It requires strong Research and Development by the local Public and private industry to use these technologies in the Civil domain and customise for the Defence with added layers of security. We still have a lot to do at the core of these technology in fabrication of future communication components and devices which require lot of investments. The 5 G and 6 G technologies will further add to the capability as well as complexity. Are we technology ready for adaptation of these technologies and compete with our neighbours in design and development of future systems? There is a need for perspective plan for 4th generation technology revolution and its deployment in Defence Forces. The pace of development is so fast and it will be a challenge for our companies to keep pace.

29. Impact of Emerging Technologies on Naval Defence

Cmde Naresh Kumar

Impact of emerging technologies on naval defence systems is very critical in the coming years.

Technology is a key enabler in modern warfare. This is borne out by the fact that weapons and sensors, Command Control and Communication Systems, power generation, power management & distribution systems, propulsion systems and machinery controls onboard platforms are extremely complex and invariable embedded with state of art technologies. The industry engaged in the design and development of these systems globally are constantly inventing and innovating to create systems with even more sophisticated capabilities and so that the cutting edge is continually maintained.

Self-reliance in defence implies that the country needs to build a robust defence industrial complex that constantly tracks and keeps pace with the emerging technologies, so as to constantly provide the best solutions to the defence forces. The amalgamation of the resources of DRDO, Defence PSUs and more recently a credible Defence Private sector Industry, has ensured that indigenisation stays in focus. The renewed emphasis, as articulated by the Govt through Aatamnirbhar Bharat, ensures that this thrust endures on local design, development and production of state of art weapons and systems in India.

Indian Navy has been one of the earliest proponents of indigenisation and has been at the forefront of this effort through its shipbuilding program since the early seventies. Most of the ships, submarines and aircraft carrier are now built in India and the country has adequate capacity to build its future fleet through our shipyards. This is particularly relevant since ships and submarines have a life of about thirty years including midlife upgrades and the Navy needs to continuously launch new construction programs to maintain and build its Fleet strength depending on the constantly evolving threat perceptions.

In recent times, the rapid pace of developments in science and technology have ushered in a stream of new technologies that are constantly adopted by

R&D organisations and industry to redesign and develop more complex systems and superior capabilities to meet new threats. In the Indian context, as far as the weapons and sensor systems are concerned, the Navy has been largely dependent upon DRDO and DPSUs. In recent times, the efforts of the private industry also have gathered momentum, in collaboration with DRDO and DPSUs to design and develop subsystems and technologies required for large and complex projects.

A naval frigate or a destroyer is undoubtedly one of the most complex platforms to design, build and operate. However, the submarine systems are even more complex because of severe space constraints and the harsh operating environments far below the sea surface. This is also the case with airborne platforms like fighter aircraft or P8I crammed with multitude of weapon & sensors for their operational roles and missions. Since the weapons and sensors on naval platforms are developed by many agencies, they need to be integrated onboard for the platform to function effectively. This requires platform level system interfacing and integration for functionality. This key requirement, to integrate many systems of diverse origin, has been developed by the Weapon and Electronics Systems Engineering Establishment (WESEE), which is the principal agency of the Navy for system integration of all platforms. WESEE has also developed critical systems like Command and Control, Data Link and the Network Centric systems in collaboration with the Indian industry.

As the Navy takes on the role of net security provider in the region, it needs to operate over extended ranges, far away from its shores and therefore needs to have an advanced communications and information network for ISR ((Intelligence, Surveillance and Reconnaissance) to enable all its ships and shore Command and Control centres to be able to exchange information in real-time through Tactical and Satellite communication links for network centric warfare.

The emerging technologies like UAVs, Satellite Communication and Surveillance, long-range precision-guided ammunition, optical and IR sensors, high energy weapons, Cyber Security, Artificial Intelligence and Data Analytics are going to define warfare tactics in the future and are examined in the succeeding paragraphs to analyse their impact on the design and development of new systems.

Unmanned Ships and Submersibles

Unmanned Surface Vessels (USVs) unmanned underwater vessels (UUVs) (Fig 29.1) and Unmanned Aerial Vehicles (UAVs) have come into sharp focus in recent times as they offer autonomous or remote-controlled operations, with the control centres being far removed from the immediate area of operations. Increasingly sophisticated systems are being designed and planned for the future by the Navies based on emerging technologies of Navigation and Communications.

It will not be long before the concept of autonomous ships gains traction and they become a part of Navy's surface fleet. Autonomous ships of the future will allow for unprecedented levels of flexibility and decentralization. Initially due to current limitations in technology it would be smaller, more distributed systems in the face of enemy threats, particularly anti-ship missiles. However, in the future It would develop into Medium Unmanned Surface Vehicles (MUSVs) which can be tasked with intelligence, surveillance and reconnaissance payloads and electronic warfare missions and Large Unmanned Surface vessels (LUSVs) could be more offensive in nature, armed with anti-ship and land-attack missiles. These platforms could be operated from other fleet ships. Some of the advanced navies have already created several platforms for testing and integrating autonomous USVs.

Fig 29.1 PC: George Town security studies review

Similarly, it will not be difficult to develop Extra Large Underwater Unmanned Vehicles (XLUUV) that could be designed to have a large endurance, operate independently with mission program run remotely. The submarine like platform could be deployed for mine countermeasures, anti-submarine warfare, anti-surface warfare, and also for strike missions. The payloads would be defined by the mission and would include sonar to detect enemy submarines and send location data to friendly helicopters and surface ships via secure Data links. They can also be equipped with Torpedoes as well as anti-ship Missiles. The modular payload system and open architecture software on such platforms can enable rapid transition and configuration based on the needs. Some of the advanced Navies have already created several platforms for testing and integrating autonomous USVs.

In the Indian context, given the increased surveillance requirements, and the limited availability of platforms, these capabilities need to be developed. In the near future, the smaller USVs may be added by the Navy to supplement its manned fleet for Surveillance and Control. Small USVs can scout around the outside of the fleet and extend the range of the radar coverage. Although airborne drones are currently used to extend the radar horizon and EW tasks, USVs could also be exploited with greater independence and endurance. The mission capability could be expanded in the future for missile delivery also.

Research and development in these areas need to be initiated and emerging design capabilities in the private sector industry harnessed to build such high-tech platforms as per the requirements of the Navy.

Satellite Networks and Command Control Systems

The future ISR shall be driven by the Fourth Industrial Revolution (4IR) technologies that are smart and intelligent, use predictive-cognitive tools and algorithms, and drive autonomous, unmanned and remote-controlled platforms, robots and machines. Some of the frontline technologies like Artificial Intelligence (AI), Machine Learning (ML), Big Data, cloud computing, Augmented Reality (AR), Quantum Computing, Cognitive Computing (CC) and Internet of Things (IoT) are gathering momentum and finding use in supporting ISR operations

Space X is already in the process of establishing space-based 5 G communications and satellite networks to provide very high bandwidth communications around the Globe. There is no doubt that these commercial technologies will find applications in defence networks especially for tracking hypersonic missiles with optical and IR sensors on the Satellite networks. Most of the data could be processed on the edge and communicated between the satellite chain and finally passed to the ships at sea.

For Network Centric Warfare, the decision support systems with smart sensors and weapons using Data Analytics and Artificial Intelligence algorithms would require a continuous upgrade of existing weapons and sensors. Integration of these technologies into weapons and sensors would require major efforts by DRDO and Defence industry, both public and private, to work in unison with the Navy. The operation and maintenance of such a complex system of system would require the naval personnel to acquire the knowledge and expertise in these highly complex new technologies and therefore will call for a major upgrade to their training infrastructure and the teaching faculty requirements to reskilling officers and sailors.

Artificial Intelligence, Data Analytics and Machine Learning

In today's fast-paced information age, individuals, companies, and government organizations are faced with a unique challenge — gaining insights amidst the explosion of inbound data. In the future, the availability of even larger volumes of data from multiple sensors and sources will be unmanageable for real-time human comprehension decision making. There is a need to use AI and develop intelligent systems that may automatically generate deep insights from different discrete decisions or inputs. The intelligent platform may increase efficiency and improve the capabilities during various unpredictive operations. The AI-enabled military infrastructure could increase the efficiency and effectiveness of the ground performances. According to the need of modern warfare the human-machine team or man-unmanned collaborations could be equipped for better control. These technologies depend upon large data and the complex algorithms to observe, correlate, extract, and predict various outcomes by optimising the processes and shall enhance system performance many folds. AI shall enable better target recognition through the correlation of vast data recorded earlier in the EW and Acoustic libraries. AI shall also have an impact on the logistics and supply chains and the reliability and maintainability of systems onboard. Technologies like 3D printing will enable the manufacture of mission-critical parts onboard or in the repair yards and Cobotics will help disassembly and assembly of complex machines in the repair centres like in the production line.

Cyber Security and Warfare

Since the over-reliance on computer networks for all transactions is a given today, it is but natural that this mass of data is targeted by many for obvious reasons of gaining from it. This has led to an increase in large-scale cyber attacks, data breaches, ransomware attacks, corporate espionage, and insider threat cases. As our adversaries adapt these methods to attack us, we need to develop advanced tools for cyber analytics and intelligence to provide an edge to overcome those threats.

We have a large pool of qualified multi-domain knowledge and interdisciplinary subject matter experts, to develop advanced data collection, processing, AI/ML-augmented analysis and visualization tools to detect and counter any threats to our communication and critical infrastructure. Navy by itself may require experts in this crucial area to work with industry and keep a 24X7 watch on our networks to identify intrusions and take corrective action on public networks.

High Energy Laser Weapons

The fibre laser technology systems have shrunk down to a level where they can fit on ground vehicles, helicopters, and ships. The beam quality of fibre lasers is excellent to deliver maximum power to the target and thus Fibre laser systems are now able to point on a distant object and disable its electronics. The second use of such weapons is as a counter to the proliferation of low-cost threats, like drones. Drones in large numbers can do a lot of damage and can simply exhaust the magazines of any current defensive weapon. Lasers can complement kinetic weapons – never running out of "bullets". Laser weapon systems have some key advantages for dealing with drone swarms. They provide the speed of light "flyout" time and can hit a target immediately. Lasers also have a very low cost per shot, so it makes sense to use them against low-cost threats like drones.

Space-Based Surveillance Systems

SpaceX just launched 60 Starlink satellites from Launch Complex 39A (LC-39A) at Kennedy Space Center in Florida. Unbounded by traditional ground infrastructure, Starlink can deliver high-speed broadband internet to locations where access has been unreliable or completely unavailable. At a time when more people are working from home and more students are participating in virtual learning, internet connectivity is more important than ever.

A space-based blanket of advanced sensors can keep "eyes always on" on the lookout for potential missile attacks. The pace of this new technology is on a near-exponential curve. The next-generation system of satellites shall provide early warning of intercontinental and ballistic missile launches with optical, infrared, Radar-based surveillance systems looking from high in the sky and covering a large area. ISRO has adequate indigenous technology to help the defence forces for constant surveillance over the entire range and can further enhance these capabilities with upcoming advances in Optical and IR sensors in lower orbit satellites.

Conclusion

As technology continues to grow by leaps and bounds there is an incessant need for adopting it to innovate and develop new systems with greater potential in the future. Technology is impacting the platforms as well as system design in numerous ways and the Navy has to embrace these developments to stay abreast. The unprecedented pace of evolution in technology needs to be harnessed with upgrades of existing systems and the development of new highly capable systems. The unmanned platforms for surface and the underwater domain will play a significant role in the next decade and such systems need to be developed for the extended role with manned platforms.

The commercial high speed 5G broadband internet services from agencies like Star link may find use in defence especially for Surveillance and tracking of Hypersonic missiles and extended ISR operations over long ranges. The extensive opportunities to use Artificial Intelligence and Data Analytics techniques in systems design and maintenance and support of systems need to explored by the local Industry. This calls for the Navy to prepare a perspective plan to embrace these technologies and place greater thrust on training its personnel to learn these technologies and also re-skill service and civilian personnel with advance training and learning management systems.

References

"Microsoft: undersea datacentres at offshore wind farms could boost web for billions", https://www.rechargenews.com/wind/microsoft-undersea-datacentres-at-offshore-wind-farms-could-boost-web-for-billions/2-1-875547 (accessed 16 October 2020).

"Growing at a slower pace, the world population is expected to reach 9.7 billion in 2050 and could peak at nearly 11 billion around 2100", https://www.un.org/development/desa/en/news/population/world-population-prospects-2019.html (accessed 16 October 2020).

"Number of internet users worldwide from 2005 to 2019", https://www.statista.com/statistics/273018/number-of-internet-users-worldwide/ (accessed 16 October 2020).

"Number of internet of things (IoT) connected devices worldwide in 2018, 2025 and 2030", https://www.statista.com/statistics/802690/worldwide-connected-devices-by-access-technology/ (accessed 16 October 2020).

"Submarine Cable Frequently Asked Questions", https://www2.telegeography.com/submarine-cable-faqs-frequently-asked-questions (accessed 16 October 2020).

"Submarine Cables and the Internet Age", https://www.ufinet.com/submarine-cables-and-the-internet-age/ (accessed 16 October 2020).

"Microsoft's undersea data center now has a webcam with fish swimming past 27.6 petabytes of data", https://www.theverge.com/tldr/2018/8/9/17669936/microsoft-undersea-datacenter-webcam (accessed 16 October 2020).

"Total Consumer Power Consumption Forecast", https://www.researchgate.net/publication/320225452_Total_Consumer_Power_Consumption_Forecast/link/59d5ee16aca2725954c78d15/download (accessed 16 October 2020).

"Underwater Data Centers", https://theliquidgrid.com/2017/10/24/underwater-data-centers/ (accessed 16 October 2020).

"The Digital Industry Is Part of the Climate Change Problem", https://disruptionhub.com/the-digital-industry-is-part-of-the-climate-change-problem/ (accessed 16 October 2020).

"Underwater Data Centers Market - Growth, Future Prospects & Competitive Analysis", https://www.credenceresearch.com/report/underwater-data-centers-market (accessed 16 October 2020).

"How the Internet Spans the Globe". https://cacm.acm.org/magazines/2020/1/241709-how-the-internet-spans-the-globe/fulltext (accessed 16 October 2020).

'The Future of Data Centers", https://www.cbinsights.com/research/future-of-data-centers/ (accessed 21 April 2020).

"How Important Is Location When Choosing a Data Center?", https://www.datacenterknowledge.com/industry-perspectives/how-important-location-when-choosing-data-center (accessed 16 October 2020).

"Floating Data Centers to be Designed for Singapore" https://www.maritime-executive.com/article/floating-data-centers-to-be-designed-for-singapore (accessed 16 October 2020).

"SpaceX just launched 60 new Starlink internet satellites and nailed rocket landing at sea", https://www.space.com/spacex-starlink-satellites-launch-rocket-landing-oct-18-2020 (accessed 24 October 2020).

"Elon Musk's 'internet from space' service coming in six month", http://timesofindia.indiatimes.com/articleshow/75356989.cms?utm_source=contentofinterest&utm_medium=text&utm_campaign=cppst (accessed 24 October 2020).

"SpaceX receives contract to build missile-tracking satellites for the Defense Department", https://www.theverge.com/2020/10/6/21503165/spacex-space-development-agency-contract-missile-warning-satellites-starlink (accessed 24 October 2020).

"SpaceX launches South Korea's 1st military satellite, nails rocket landing at sea", https://www.space.com/spacex-launches-south-korean-military-satellite-anasis-2-lands-rocket.html (accessed 24 October 2020).

"Wild Wide Web: Consequences of Digital Fragmentation", https://reports.weforum.org/global-risks-report-2020/wild-wide-web/#view/fn-11 (accessed 24 October 2020)

https://www.imdb.com/title/tt9263550/

https://dras.in/frontier-to-outer-space/

https://dras.in/climate-change-and-the-oceans/

https://www.researchgate.net/figure

https://www.nationalgeographic.org/

https://www.eia.gov/energyexplained/hydropower

https://hu.pinterest.com/pin/448248969163303839/

https://www.geoenergymarketing.com/energy-blog/potential-offshore-geother mal-resources/

https://dras.in/lethal-autonomous-weapon-systems-a-challenge-to-humanity/

https://www.unidir.org/

https://www.republicworld.com/india-news/general-news/bel-signs-contract-with-indian-navy-to-supply-laser-dazzlers.html

https://dras.in/military-lasers-a-future-market-perspective/

https://www.laserfocusworld.com/lasers-sources/article/16569327/lifi-replacing-wifi-multipointtomultipointcapable-optical-data-transmission-for-automation

https://www.extremetech.com/extreme/128207-1gbps-wireless-network-made-with-red-and-green-laser-pointers

https://www.extremetech.com/extreme/128207-1gbps-wireless-network-made-with-red-and-green-laser-pointers

https://www.securitytoday.in/indian-news/drdo-showcases-vehicle-mounted-laser-dazzler-for-crowd-control/

https://www.photonicsonline.com/doc/russia-developing-plane-mounted-lasers-to-blast-satellites-us-confirms-deployment-of-vehicle-mounted-anti-drone-lasers-0001

https://defence-blog.com/news/russia-develops-advanced-anti-satellite-aircraft-mounted-laser.html

https://www.electronicsforu.com/technology-trends/less-lethal-laser-weapons/3

https://www.waves.intec.ugent.be/research/wireless-body-area-networks

https://dras.in/smart-couture-customized-military-clothing/

https://dras.in/disruptive-technologies-for-indias-military-might-part-1-of-2/

https://dras.in/swarm-technology-in-drones-towards-self-reliance/

https://en.wikipedia.org/wiki/Active_electronically_scanned_array

https://en.wikipedia.org/wiki/Electronic_counter-countermeasure

https://en.wikipedia.org/wiki/Electronic_warfare_support_measures

https://www.goodreads.com/quotes/tag/drone-attacks

https://foreignpolicy.com/2020/10/15/drones-tanks-obsolete-nagorno-karabakh-azerbaijan-armenia/

https://www.mydronelab.com/blog/types-of-military-drones.html

https://www.darpa.mil/program/fast-lightweight-autonomy

https://www.roboticsbusinessreview.com/unmanned/small-drones-military-surveillance/

https://en.wikipedia.org/wiki/Synthetic-aperture_radar

https://www.defenseone.com/technology/2016/02/militarys-super-fast-bird-drone/125938/

https://en.wikipedia.org/wiki/Synthetic-aperture_radar

https://www.defenseone.com/technology/2016/02/militarys-super-fast-bird-drone/125938/

https://www.usni.org/magazines/proceedings/2014/february/bring-countermeasure-drones

https://www.usni.org/magazines/proceedings/2014/february/bring-countermeasure-drones

https://www.ovzon.com/en/drone-operations/

https://www.intechopen.com/chapters/56737

https://www.thehindu.com/news/international/amazon-wins-faa-approval-to-deliver-packages-by-drone/article32493457.ece

http://www.indiandefencereview.com/news/drone-swarms-the-emerging-air-threat/

https://www.newscientist.com/article/2227168-turkey-is-getting-military-drones-armed-with-machine-guns/

http://defencejournal.com/2000/sept/military.htm

https://www.japcc.org/unmanned-air-systems-in-nato-anti-submarine-warfare-asw/

https://dronelife.com/2020/06/18/nano-drones-the-tiny-drones-the-military-is-buying/

https://digitalsky.dgca.gov.in/home

https://www.commercialuavnews.com/infrastructure/india-opens-the-sky-for-drones-under-no-permission-no-takeoff-npnt-system

https://www.militaryaerospace.com/computers/article/

https://breakingdefense.com/2019/10/artificial-intelligence-will-detect-hidden-targets-in-2020-wargame/

https://breakingdefense.com/2018/11/army-ai-task-force-comes-to-pittsburgh-c-o-cmu/

https://sonix.ai/articles/difference-between-artificial-intelligence-machine-learning-and-natural-language-processing/

https://www.orfonline.org/expert-speak/artificial-intelligence-military-operations-where-does-india-stand-54030/

https://www.marketsandmarkets.com/Market-Reports/artificial-intelligence-military-market-41793495.html

https://usiofindia.org/publication/usi-journal/artificial-intelligence-in-military-operations-technology-and-ethics-indian-perspective/

https://thebulletin.org/2018/04/the-promise-and-peril-of-military-applications-of-artificial-intelligence/

https://analyticsindiamag.com/indias-plan-on-laws-showcases-that-it-wants-to-play-a-bigger-role-in-the-ai-arms-race/

https://iiot-world.com/artificial-intelligence/five-challenges-in-designing-a-fully-autonomous-system-for-driverless-cars/

https://blogs.ubc.ca/wberry301/best-work/definitions-of-fully-autonomous-systems/

https://www.reachingcriticalwill.org/resources/fact-sheets/critical-issues/7972-fully-autonomous-weapons

https://www.armscontrol.org/act/2019-03/features/autonomous-weapons-systems-laws-war

https://www.researchgate.net/publication/331866114 - algorithmsappliedin autonomousvehiclesystems

Algorithmic Warfare Applying Artificial Intelligence to Warfighting by LAYTON PETER (2018).

The U.S. military, algorithmic warfare, and big tech by Khari Johnson (2019)

https://www.nationaldefensemagazine.org/articles/2019/7/2/algorithmic-warfare-darpas-ai-next-program-bearing-fruit

https://websitebuilders.com/blog/algorithmic-warfare/

https://venturebeat.com/2019/11/08/the-u-s-military-algorithmic-warfare-and-big-tech/

https://www.weforum.org/agenda/2018/09/algorithmic-war-is-coming-humans-must-retain-control/

https://smallwarsjournal.com/jrnl/art/emerging-capability-military-applications-artificial-intelligence-and-machine-learning

https://www.researchgate.net/publication/326248009_Algorithmic_Warfare_Applying_Artificial_Intelligence_to_Warfighting

Kamhawi. H, Arrington. IA, et al. 'Performance evaluation of a High Energy Pulsed Plasma Thruster' AIAA- 2005-3695. 41st Joint Propulsion Conference, Tuscon, AZ, July 2005

T. Froehlich, "RITA, High-Efficiency Long Life Radio Frequency Ion Thruster". EADS International Technology Conference 2003, Paris, France.

H. Bassner et al, "Development Steps of RF Ion Thruster- RIT -37th Joint Propulsion Conference and Exhibition"-2001, Salt Lake City, Utah.

Kazuo. S, "Magnetic Levitation Technologies: Railway Technology Today"- Review pp 58-60. www.rtri.or.jp

Gallant, E. Vanderbeke et al, "Design Considerations for an Electromagnetic Railgun to be used against anti ship missiles" IEEE Transactions on Plasma Science Vol 41, No 10, pp 2800-2804, 2013.

Ministry of Defence, GoI, Defence Research and Development Organisation. (2020, September 07). DRDO successfully flight tests Hypersonic Technology Demonstrator Vehicle [Press release]. Retrieved September 7, 2020, from https://www.pib.gov.in/PressReleasePage.aspx?PRID=1651956

J.R., W. (2019, May 01). The emerging world of hypersonic weapons technology. Retrieved September 07, 2020, from https://www.militaryaerospace.com/power/article/14033431/the-emerging-world-of-hypersonic-weapons-technology

Judson, J. (2020, August 05). How the DoD plans to meet its ambitious hypersonic missile test schedule. Retrieved September 07, 2020, from https://www.defensenews.com/digital-show-dailies/smd/2020/08/05/heres-how-the-dod-plans-to-meet-its-ambitious-hypersonic-missile-test-schedule/

Edwards, Sean J. Swarming and the Future of Warfare. RAND Corp Santa Monica CA, 2005.

Arquilla, John, and David Ronfeldt. Swarming and the Future of Conflict. No. RAND/D8-311-OSD. RAND Corp Santa Monica CA, 2000.

Pant, Atul. Aerial Drones In Future Wars: A Conceptual Perspective. Occasional Paper. Manohar Parrikar Institute for Defence Studies and Analyses, 2020.

Narang RK. UAV Swarms: China's Leap In Cutting-edge Technologies. Air Power Journal Vol. 13 No. 3, Monsoon 2018 (July-September) pp. 59-81.

Reynolds, Craig W. "Flocks, herds and schools: A distributed behavioral model." Proceedings of the 14th annual conference on Computer graphics and interactive techniques. 1987.

Ren, Wei, and Randal W. Beard. Distributed consensus in multi-vehicle cooperative control. Vol. 27. No. 2. London: Springer London, 2008.

Rossi, Federico, et al. "Review of multi-agent algorithms for collective behavior: a structural taxonomy." IFAC-PapersOnLine 51.12 (2018): 112-117.

Joshi, Apurva. Experiments in modelling and control of multi-agent systems. Ph.D. Thesis, IIT Bombay, Monash University, 2019.

Borkar, Aseem. Surveillance and Monitoring Strategies for Autonomous Mobile Agents. Ph.D. Thesis, IIT Bombay, 2019.

Reddit is an American social news aggregation, web content rating, and discussion website, where registered members submit content to the site such as links, text posts, and images, which are then voted up or down by other members. Posts are organized by subject into user-created boards called "subreddits", which cover a variety of topics including news, science, movies, video games, music, books, fitness, food, and image-sharing. Submissions with more up-votes appear towards the top of their subreddit and, if they receive enough votes, ultimately on the site's front page. As of March 2019, Reddit had 542 million monthly visitors (234 million unique users), ranking as the No. 6 most visited website in U.S. and No. 21 in the world

Pavel Korshunov and Sebastien Marcel; DeepFakes: a New Threat to Face Recognition? Assessment and Detection

https://arxiv.org/abs/1905.08233, Egor Zakharov, Aliaksandra Shysheya, Egor-Burkov, Victor Lempitsky, Few-Shot Adversarial Learning of Realistic Neural Talking Head Models

"Raksha Mantri Shri Rajnath Singh Launches Naval Innovation and Indigenisation Organisation (NIIO)", https://pib.gov.in/PressReleseDetailm.aspx-?PRID=1645549 [3] (accessed 13 August 2020).

"Indian Navy inks deal with UPEIDA govt for setting up centre of excellence", https://www.livemint.com/news/india/indian-navy-inks-deal-with-upeida-govt-for-setting-up-centre-of-excellence-11597370306749.html [4] (accessed 15 August 2020).

"RSU inks MoU with Indian Navy for capacity building, research projects", https://timesofindia.indiatimes.com/india/rsu-inks-mou-with-indian-navy-for-capacity-building-research-projects/articleshowprint/77532161.cms [5] (accessed 14 August 2020).

"Indian Naval Indigenisation Plan (INIP) 2015-2030", https://ddpmod.gov.in/sites/default/files/INIP%20(2015-2030).pdf (accessed 15 august 2020). Also see "Indian Naval Indigenisation Plan (INIP) 2015-2030", https://www.indiannavy.nic.in/content/indian-naval-indigenisation-plan-inip-2015-2030 [6] (accessed 15 August 2020).

"Interview with the CNS", https://www.defstrat.com/magazine_articles/interview-with-the-cns/(accessed 15 August 2020).

"AIoT: When Artificial Intelligence Meets the Internet of Things", https://www.visualcapitalist.com/aiot-when-ai-meets-iot-technology/ [7] (accessed 14 August 2020).

"Rajnath Singh approves Rs 400-crore defence testing infrastructure scheme",https://www.business-standard.com/article/economy-policy/rajnath-singh-approves-rs-400-crore-defence-testing-infrastructure-scheme-120051600065_1.html (accessed 15 August 2020).

Vijay Sakhuja, "Indian Navy: Time to Explore Drone Motherships" https://www.vifindia.org/2020/may/26/indian-navy-time-to-explore-drone-motherships [8] (accessed 15 August 2020).

Binford Research Labs Pvt Ltd (www.binford.io)

Analyzing the Threat of Unmanned Aerial Vehicles (UAV) to Nuclear Facilities by Alexander Solodov, Adam Williams, Sara Al Hanaei, Braden Goddard

Esteban Tlelo-Cuautle Esteban, Jan 2012, Researchgate, VLSI Design (DOI: 10.5772/2255)

Retrieved from: https://www.researchgate.net/publication/234007956_VLSI_Design, Accessed on 13-14 Apr 2021

Kim Ho Yeap Kim Ho, Nisar Humaira, 29 Sep 2016, intechopen, VLSI (DOI: 10.5772/intechopen.69188), Retrieved from: https://www.intechopen.com/books/very-large-scale-integration/introductory-chapter-vlsi,Accessed on 13-14 Apr 2021

informIT, 18 Feb 2018, informIT (Pearson), Digital Systems and VLSI, Retrieved from:

https://www.informit.com/articles/article.aspx?p=1315269, Accessed on 13-14 Apr 2021

Cadence PCB Solutions, ND, cadence.com, VLSI Technology: Its History and Uses in Modern Technology, Retrieved From: https://resources.pcb.cadence.com/blog/2020-vlsi-technology-its-history-and-uses-in-modern-technology, Accessed on 13-14 Apr 2021

Bryant Randal E, Cheng KTT, Kahng A, Keutzer Kurt, Maly Wojciech P, Newton R, Pileggi L. Rabaey J.M , Sangiovanni-Vincentelli Alberto L, Resaerchgate, Limitations and challenges of computer-aided design technology for CMOS VLSI (DOI:10.1109/5.915378), Retrieved From: https://www.researchgate.net/publication/2985818_Limitations_and_challenges_of_computer-aided_design_technology_for_CMOS_VLSI, Accessed on 13-14 Apr 2021

Cadence PCB Solutions, NDa, cadence.com, VLSI Technology: Its History and

Uses in Modern Technology, Retrieved From: https://resources.pcb.cadence.com/blog/2020-vlsi-technology-its-history-and-uses-in-modern-technology, Accessed on 13-14 Apr 2021

Kumar SeelamVasavi Sai Viswanada Prabhu Deva, 04 Dec 2017, slideshare, Very Large Scale Integration (VLSI) technology, Retrieved from: https://www.slideshare.net/SeelamVasaviSaiViswa/very-large-scale-integration-vlsi-technology, Accessed on 13-14 Apr 2021

Shidling Chetan, 04 Nov 2020, cselectricalandelectronics, Roadmap To Becoming A VLSI Engineer Or Chips Design Engineer, Retrieved From: https://www.cselectricalandelectronics.com/roadmap-to-becoming-a-vlsi-engineer-or-chips-design-engineer/, Accessed on 13-14 Apr 2021

Siddamal Saroja V, ShirolSuhas, Hiremath Shraddha, Iyer Nalini. Jan 2020, Reserachgate, Towards Sustainable Integrated Model for Skill Development: A Collaborative Approach (DOI:10.1016/j.procs.2020.05.099), Retrieved From: https://www.researchgatc.net/publication/342226259_Towards_Sustainable_Integrated_Model_for_Skill_Development_A_Collaborative_Approach, Accessed on 13-14 Apr 2021

Phadnis Shilpa and John Sujit, 14 Apr 2021, Times of India Print Edition, Why India needs a lot more talent that can craft Chips, Accessed through Print edition on 14 Apr 2021.

Cassidy Sean, 21 Nov 2016, Stanford University, Pulse Detonation Engines, Retrieved from: http://large.stanford.edu/courses/2016/ph240/cassady1/#:~:text=The%20Pulse%20Detonation%20Engine%20(PDE,efficiency%20and%20reduced%20mechanical%20complexity , Accessed on 10-11 Apr 2021

Aerodynamics Research Center, 2014, University of Taxa Arlington, Pulsed Detonation Engines, Retrieved from: https://arc.uta.edu/research/pde.htm, Accessed on 10-11 Apr 2021

Cassidy Sean, 21 Nov 2016a, Stanford University, Pulse Detonation Engines, Retrieved from: http://large.stanford.edu/courses/2016/ph240/cassady1/#:~:text=The%20Pulse%20Detonation%20Engine%20(PDE,efficiency%20and%20reduced%20mechanical%20complexity , Accessed on 10-11 Apr 2021

Pandey KM and Debnath Pinku Dr, Jan 2016, Researchgate (Article in Journal of Combustion), Review on Recent Advances in Pulse Detonation Engines (DOI: 10.1155/2016/4193034) Retrieved from: https://www.researchgate.net/publication/291205810_Review_on_Recent_Advances_in_Pulse_Detonation_Engines, accessed on 10-11 Apr 2021

Bulat Pavel Viktorovich, Aug 2014, Researchgate, About the Detonation Engines, DOI:10.3844/ajassp.2014.1357.1364), Retrieved from: https://www.researchgate.net/publication/263651647_About_the_detonation_engine

Valli DM and Jindal TK Dr, Apr 2014, Researchgate, Pulse Detonation Engine: Parameters Affecting Performance, Retrieved from: https://www.researchgate.net/publication/268740511_Pulse_Detonation_Engine_Parameters_Affecting_Performance, Accessed on 10-11 Apr 2021

Shaw Ian J, Kildare Jordan A C, Evans Michael J, Chinnici Alfonso, Sparks Ciaran AM, Rubaiyat Shekh N.H, Chin Rey C and Medwell, Paul R,23 Oct 2018, intechopen, A Theoretical Review of Rotating Detonation Engines (DOI: 10.5772/intechopen.90470) , Retrieved from: https://www.intechopen.com/books/direct-numerical-simulations-an-introduction-and-applications/a-theoretical-review-of-rotating-detonation-engines, Accessed on 10-11 Apr 2021

India Defence News, 10 Apr 2021, indiadefnecnews, Russia's Demos Pulse Detonation Engine, Retrieved From: http://www.indiandefensenews.in/2021/04/russias-demos-pulse-detonation-engine.html , Accessed on 10-11 Apr 2021

Defence World, 20 May 2017, Defenceworld.net, India Develops Pulse Detonation Engine For Cruise, Anti-Tank Missiles, Retrieved from: https://www.defense-world.net/news/19350/India_Develops_Pulse_Detonation_Engine_For_Cruise__Anti_Tank_Missiles#.YHLZTugzbIU, Accessed on 10-11 Apr 2021

"Autonomous Ships Market worth $13.8 billion by 2030 | CAGR of 7.00%", https://www.wfmj.com/story/42537275/autonomous-ships-market-worth-138-billion-by-2030-cagr-of-700 (accessed 03 November 2020).

"Construction of Yara Birkeland Paused", https://www.maritime-executive.com/article/construction-of-yara-birkeland-paused (accessed 03 November 2020).

"MUNIN", http://www.unmanned-ship.org/munin/ (accessed 03 November 2020).

"MOL Launches R & D on Autonomous Ocean Transport System- Selected for Japanese Government Transportation Research Program", https://www.mol.co.jp/en/pr/2017/17031.html(accessed 24 September 2020).

"Japan aims to launch self-piloting ships by 2025", https://asia.nikkei.com/Tech-Science/Tech/Japan-aims-to-launch-self-piloting-ships-by-2025(accessed 24 September 2020).

"China starts building its 1st autonomous feeder", https://www.offshore-energy.biz/china-starts-building-its-1st-autonomous-feeder/ (accessed 20 May 2020).

"ProMare", https://www.ibm.com/case-studies/promare-systems-hardware-power-ai-edge (accessed 18 October 2020).

"Autonomous Ships Timeline – Comparing Rolls-Royce, Kongsberg, Yara and More",https://emerj.com/ai-adoption-timelines/autonomous-ships-timeline/(accessed 24 September 2020).

"Seafarers and digital disruption", https://www.ics-shipping.org/docs/default-source/resources/ics-study-on-seafarers-and-digital-disruption.pdf?sfvrsn=3 (accessed 30 June 2020).

http://ficci.in/events/22716/ISP/4-Nikos-Ghikas.pdf Netcentric Naval warfare through Data Links

https://economictimes.indiatimes.com/news/defence. CCS clears Rs-7796-crore-communication -network-for-indian-Army

https://www.stl.tech/blog/varun-in-the-service-of-the-nation/ Indian Navy project Varun

http://forceindia.net/cover-story/bigger-impact/ The IAF's shift to IACCS is a major step towards Net Centric Warfare

https://www.heritage.org/defense/commentary/meet-the-us-navys-unmanned-ships-the-future

https://www.raytheonintelligenceandspace.com/news/feature/eyes-argus

https://www.spacex.com/launches/

Index

F

G

H

I

J

K

L

M

Colour Plates

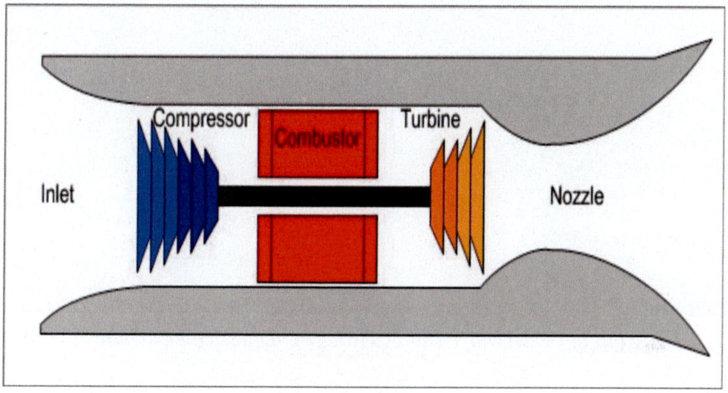

Fig 1.1 Conventional Turbo Jet Engine - Image Courtesy: Aerodynamics Research Center, University of Texas (Pg. 2)

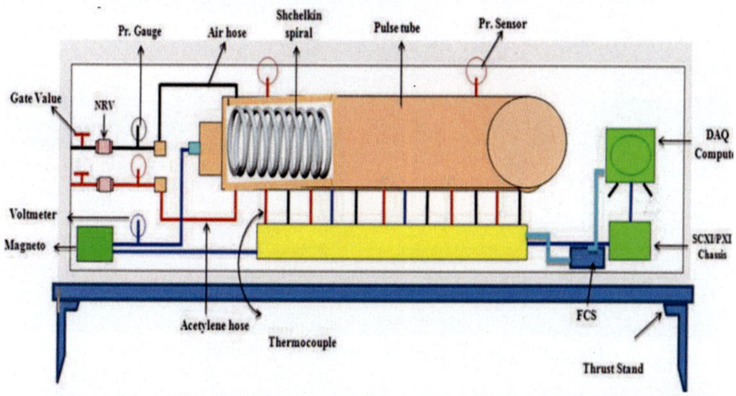

Fig: 1.2: Simplified schematic layout of PDE system - Image Courtesy: ResearchGate (Pg. 2)

Fig: 1.4 - DRDO Developed PDE - Image Courtesy: Defence World (Pg. 8)

Fig 2.1 Lay out of Underwater Data Centre (PC-Data center dynamics) (Pg. 9)

Fig 2.2 Microsoft UW data centre PC- Youtube (Pg.10)

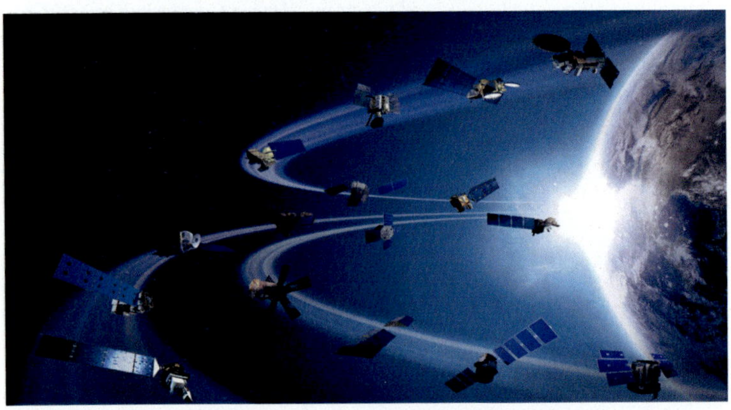

Fig 3.1 Starlink Satellites PC:Flying Magazine (Pg. 13)

Fig 3.1 Launch Pad PC: SpaceX (Pg. 14)

Fig 4.1a 1U satellite (10x10x10 Cms) (Pg. 17)

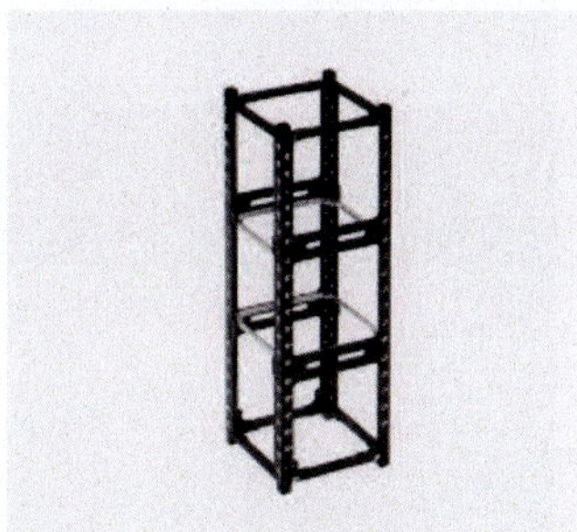

Fig 4.1b 3U frame (10X10X30 Cms) (Pg. 17)

Fig 4.2 Solar Sail Propulsion PC: Tech Crunch (Pg. 19)

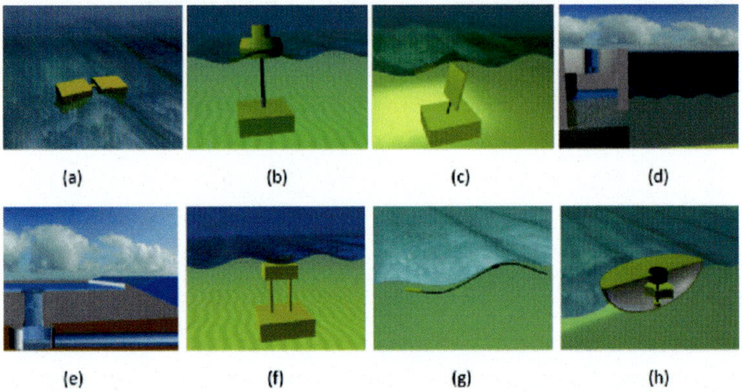

Fig 5.1 (a) attenuator (b) point absorber (c) oscillating wave surge converter (d) oscillating water column (e) over-topping device (f) submerged pressure differential (g) bulge wave (h) rotating mass. PC: Research Gate (Pg. 23)

Fig 5.2 Tidal Energy Generation PC: The Cool Down (Pg. 24)

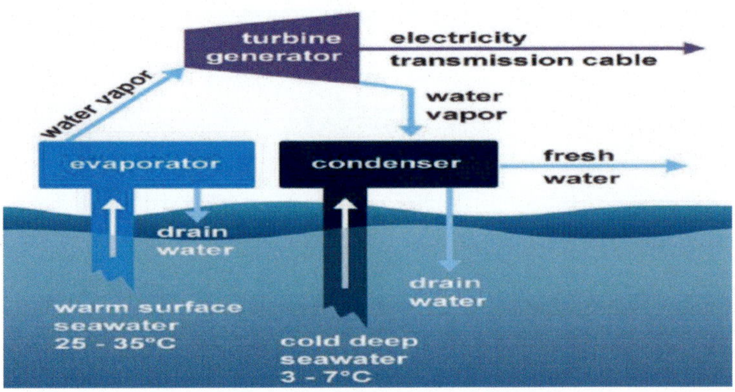

Fig 5.3 OTEC PC: EIA (Pg. 25)

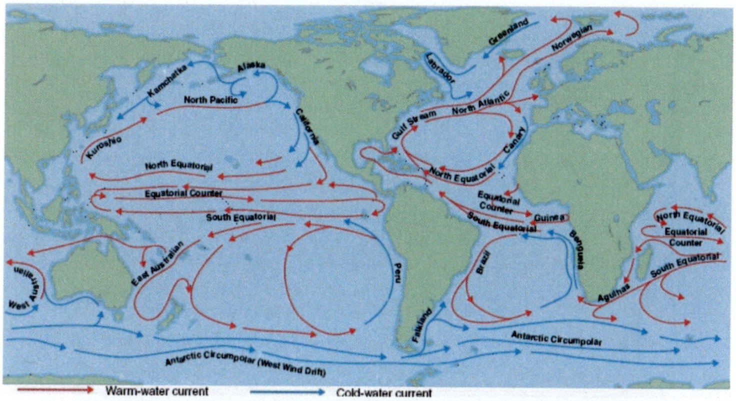

Fig 5.4 Major Ocean Currents PC: Drishti IAS (Pg.25)

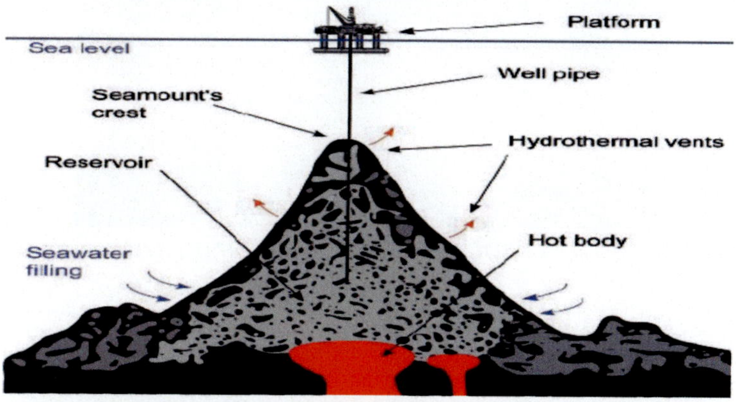

Fig 5.5 Submarine Thermal Vents PC ; Geo energy marketing (Pg. 26)

Fig 6.1 Ground Target Destruction PC: New Atlas (Pg. 29)

Fig 8.1 Autonomous Missile launching PC: Science 2.0 (Pg. 37)

Fig 9.1 DRDO Laser Gun PC: ADDA247 (Pg. 42)

Fig 11.1 Wearables -Soldier PC:Research gate (Pg. 53)

Fig 12. 1 Defending Drones PC: Military.com (Pg. 60)

Fig 13.1 DAPRA UCAV PC:Eurasia Review (Pg. 65)

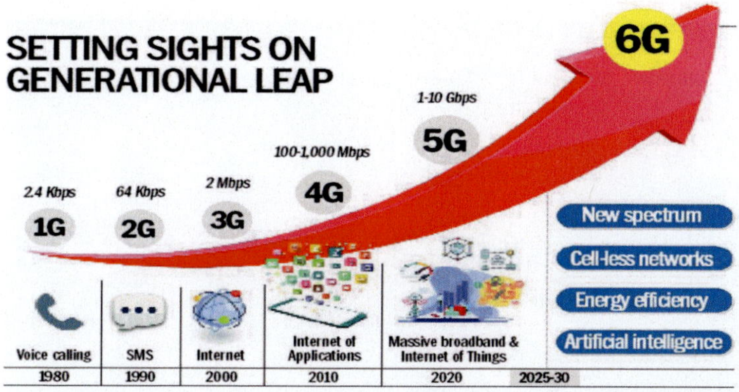

Fig17.1 PC :www.tribuneindia.com/news/comment/mission-6g (Pg 88)

Fig 20.1 PC:sputnik news (Pg. 104)

Fig 20.2 PC: warfare sims (Pg. 106)

Fig: 21. 2- Complex PCB Design, Image Courtesy: pcb.cadence (Pg. 112)